Afghan Wheels and Tracks

UK and US Vehicles

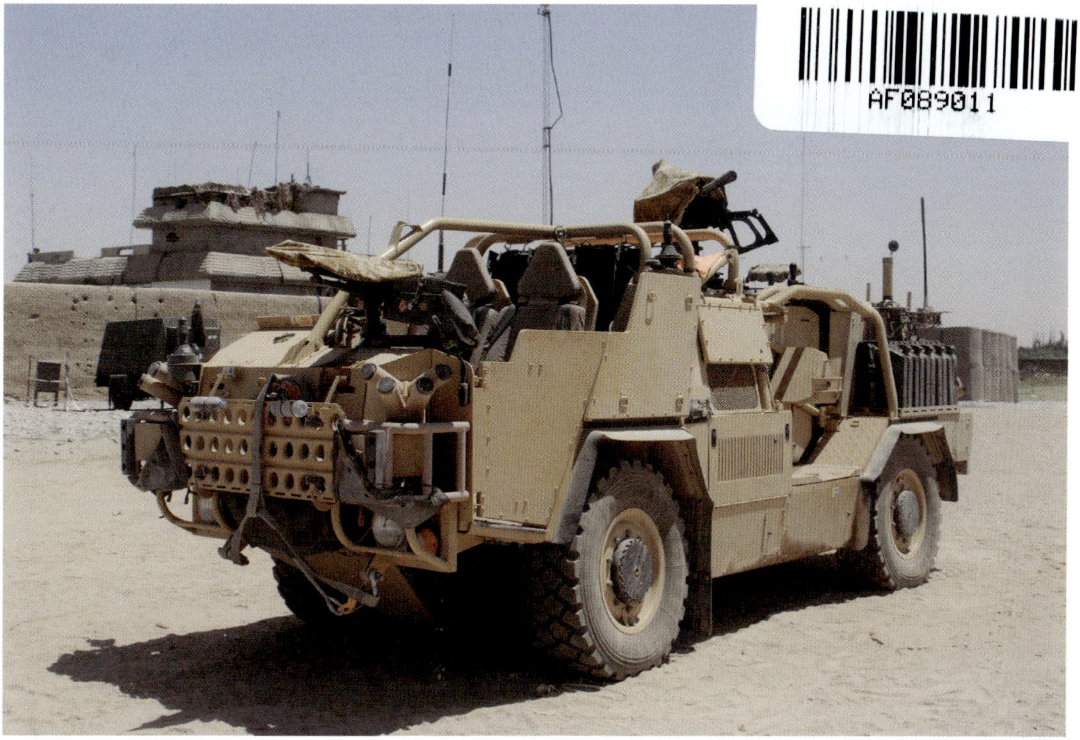

Craig Allen

KEY Books

MILITARY VEHICLES AND ARTILLERY SERIES, VOLUME 6

Front cover image: A Scimitar CVRT supporting Paratroopers on patrol in Helmand.

Back cover image: A 2 Para R-WMIK on patrol in the Sangin Valley in 2008.

Title page image: A Jackal pictured at the Forward Operating Base (FOB) at Sangin in 2008.

Contents page image: The Coyote TSV has now found a permanent place in the British military inventory supporting the Jackal 2. (Andrew Linnett, OGL v1.0OGL v1.0, via Wikimedia Commons)

Published by Key Books
An imprint of Key Publishing Ltd
PO Box 100
Stamford
Lincs PE9 1XQ

www.keypublishing.com

The right of Craig Allen to be identified as the author of this book has been asserted in accordance with the Copyright, Designs and Patents Act 1988 Sections 77 and 78.

Copyright © Craig Allen, 2022

ISBN 978 1 80282 470 4

Unless otherwise stated, all images belong to the author.

All rights reserved. Reproduction in whole or in part in any form whatsoever or by any means is strictly prohibited without the prior permission of the Publisher.

Typeset by SJmagic DESIGN SERVICES, India.

Contents

Introduction 4

Chapter 1 UK Vehicles 5

Chapter 2 US Vehicles 61

Chapter 3 Aftermath 85

Chapter 4 Operation *Pitting*, Escape from Kabul 87

Introduction

The war in Afghanistan is usually thought of as an 'infantryman's war', with Western troops battling Taliban fighters in the fields and ditches of Helmand. However, there was another side to the conflict, which created a whole new class of armoured vehicles: the so-called Protected Patrol Vehicles (PPVs). These PPVs were a response to the insurgents' wide-scale use of Improvised Explosive Devices (IEDs) and were based on earlier designs developed in Rhodesia and South Africa. Produced rapidly to meet urgent operational requirements, they also included variants for moving stores around the battlefield, as well as troops. The conflict also gave a new lease of life to some older Cold War designs, while other vehicles were found wanting in the tough operational conditions experienced in Afghanistan. With few proper roads, the rugged terrain of the Afghan backcountry also threw up the need for reconnaissance vehicles with long-range and impressive cross-country performance. Additionally, the task of supporting the fighting troops required a major logistics effort to supply the Forward Operating Bases (FOBs). This prompted the formation of the Combat Logistic Patrols (CLPs) formed from a mixture of heavy load carriers and support vehicles. The logistics war is perhaps an untold story of the conflict, along with the vehicles developed to support it. In this book, I will introduce the reader to the types in use by UK and US forces. While I make no claim to a comprehensive list, I will cover all the major vehicles along with a few lesser-known types. Post-conflict, some of these designs remain in the inventory, while others have been withdrawn as being unsuitable for conventional operations. The final withdrawal from Afghanistan in 2021 also left large amounts of Western equipment in the hands of the Taliban.

Craig Allen

A Vector 6x6 pictured at a Forward Operating Base (FOB) in Helmand.

Chapter 1
UK Vehicles

Protected Patrol Vehicles (PPVs)

The WMIK Land Rover

The Weapons Mount Installation Kit (WMIK) is the name of the first factory-produced Reconnaissance Land Rover to be taken into British service, manufactured from 1999. The WMIK was manufactured with assistance from Ricardo Engineering and based on the standard Wolf TUM 110. Inspired by the US Army's Ranger Special Operations Vehicle (RSOV), it featured a strengthened chassis and combined roll cage and rear ring mount for weapons. Designed for reconnaissance and fire support, it could initially be equipped with a General Purpose Machine Gun (GPMG), Heavy Machine Gun (HMG) or a Milan Anti-Tank System, with an additional GPMG for the commander. It was a massive step forward from the workshop-modified vehicles that came before. Powered by the standard 300TDI engine from the Wolf, it could reach 70mph (160kph) on road and weighed 3.35 tons. These WMIKs acquitted themselves well in the harsh desert conditions of southern Iraq in 2003, and for the lightly equipped Paratroopers, these well-armed and highly mobile Land Rovers proved a game-changer. Available in significant numbers, they equipped the Patrol, Machine Gun and Anti-Tank Platoons and were employed for reconnaissance, patrolling and escort duties. In the insurgency following the war, however, the increasing use of IEDs first hinted at the vehicle's vulnerability. 16 Air Assault Brigade first deployed to Afghanistan in 2006 and took its WMIK Land Rovers with it. However, several WMIKs were soon lost to IEDs and small arms fire, and something had to be done – quickly. As an interim fix, flexible kevlar panels were applied to vulnerable points on the vehicle. A more effective solution came in the form of the E(Enhanced)-WMIK, which was first deployed in 2007. This featured a Modular Armour Protection Installation Kit (MAPIK), essentially a soft-armour package, with additional underbelly protection. A full Bowman radio fit was also introduced, comprising 2 x HF and 1 x VHF sets, pushing the all-up weight to 4.1 tons. Thus, while providing extra protection, the extra weight of the armour did not help the vehicles' cross-country ability in the Afghan hinterland, which was already an issue given the WMIK's narrow tyres.

Next, a new and improved model, the R(Refurbished)-WMIK, began to reach the troops in late 2007. This re-engineered version came with enhanced blast and mine protection, the underbelly armour was now incorporated into the chassis rather than a simple bolt-on. Meanwhile, an uprated suspension system featured ARB 'locker diffs' to provide a more stable firing platform. Alloy wheels were also now fitted complete with run-flat tyres. Despite these developments, operational experience drove the need for even further modifications, which lead to the product-improved R-WMIK+. Built as new vehicles from the ground up on Wolf chassis by Land Rover and Ricardo Engineering, this final version featured a wide range of enhancements. Firstly, the body was widened, and uprated suspension was fitted along with a new heavy-duty rear axle. The 300TDI engine was uprated from 2.5 to 2.8 litres and now drove through a 4-speed ZF automatic gearbox. The combined roll cage and weapon mount were modified for extra roll-over protection, and a composite armour protection package was fitted, including armoured doors. Extra seating now allowed for a fourth crewman, but the all-up weight had increased to 4.7 tons. The R-WMIK+ began to be delivered from 2010 onwards, but once again was not without its problems. The uprated engines had a tendency to overheat, and the increase in weight led to gearbox failures and reliability issues, pointing to the fact that the limits of the design had probably been reached. This was recognised by the British military, and the R-WMIK and R-WMIK+ were effectively replaced by the newly developed Jackal in front-line use. In recent years, the R-WMIK has been re-adapted by the Parachute Regiment for its air portability, which suits the rapid-reaction role.

WMIK Specifications	
Model	WMIK
Manufacturer	Land Rover/Ricardo
Country	UK
Year	1999
Engine	300TDI; 2.5 litre; 111hp
Fuel	Diesel
Transmission	5-speed manual
Suspension	4x4
Top Speed	70mph on road
Range	350 miles
Armament	7.62 GPMG or 12.7 HMG
Crew Capacity	3
Weight	3.5 tons

Above left: An R-WMIK armed with an HK 40mm General Machine Gun (GMG), pictured on a recent exercise with the Parachute Regiment. (16 Air Assault Brigade)

Above right: An R-WMIK carries out a clearance patrol in Helmand. Note the vigilance of the crew and the recovery strop pre-fitted to the towing pintle.

The commander's position. Note the raised seat to offer an improved arc for the GPMG and ballistic panel in the door space.

An R-WMIK on patrol in Helmand. Note the typical crew stowage and the hessian screens for the lights and radiator. (16 Air Assault Brigade)

The R-WMIK+ during an exercise in the UK. This ultimate version featured heavier armour, pushing the design to its limits and sadly causing reliability issues.

The Snatch Land Rover

The Snatch Land Rover was originally designed for use as a patrol vehicle in Northern Ireland in the early 1990s to replace the earlier ad-hoc Land Rover types with bolt-on protection kits. It was based on the heavy-duty Wolf 110 chassis and was developed with the aid of the Ricardo engineering company. The composite armoured body offered only limited protection from blasts, and the vehicle was never intended to withstand powerful explosive devices. In fact, it wasn't even employed in the hard areas of West Belfast, where better-protected Armoured Patrol Vehicles (APV) Land Rovers were used instead. Nevertheless, the Snatch found itself in front-line use in Iraq and Afghanistan on the basis it was all that was available at the time. Tragically, this led to several fatalities, as the vehicles fell victim to roadside bombs and IEDs. The resulting media coverage soon gave the Snatch the notorious nickname of 'mobile coffin', whereas in truth it was simply miss-employed. However, the Snatch saga did lead to an urgent operational requirement for better-protected patrol vehicles.

As already noted, the Snatch was essentially a Wolf 110 with composite Vehicle Protection Kit (VPK). The vehicle was originally powered by a V8 engine, although in later versions this was replaced by a 300TDI. With a two-man crew and the ability to carry up to four dismounts, a roof hatch enabled one or two soldiers to act as top cover. Armament relied on the troops' personal weapons or a GPMG on its bipod, and the Snatch was useful for patrolling in low-threat environments. For use in Afghanistan, air conditioning and electronic counter-measures (ECM) were fitted, but the vehicle was withdrawn once better-protected types such as the Foxhound became available.

Snatch Specifications	
Model	Snatch (CAV 100)
Manufacturer	Land Rover/Ricardo
Country	UK
Year	2006
Engine	3.9 V8 or 300TDI
Fuel	Petrol/Diesel
Transmission	5-speed manual
Suspension	4x4
Top Speed	60mph
Range	320 miles
Armament	Personal weapons
Crew Capacity	2+4
Weight	3.9 tons

On patrol in Afghanistan. The high prevalence of IEDs made the lightly armoured Snatch unsuitable for this role. (British MOD, Open Government Licence)

UK Vehicles

Above left: On the streets of Basrah. It was here in Iraq that the vulnerability of the Snatch Land Rover was first revealed. (British MOD, Open Government Licence)

Above right: Snatches operating in Afghanistan. Note the proliferation of antennas and the snorkel air intake to reduce dust ingestion. (British MOD, Open Government Licence)

Right: A Snatch pictured in the UK beside an R-WMIK+. Note the antenna boxes on the wings and the desert camouflage net covering the body. (British MOD, Open Government Licence)

A rear view displaying the crew door and small armoured windows. Note the toughened Perspex protecting the top cover position. (British MOD, Open Government Licence)

Above: The Snatch in classic Northern Ireland configuration. The vehicle was never designed to operate in high-threat areas. (British MOD, Open Government Licence)

Left: A 'Desert Snatch' pictured at an equipment exhibition. Note the heavy-duty window screens, raised air intake and 'wire cutter' attachment. (British MOD, Open Government Licence)

Vector PPV

The Vector is an armoured version of the 6x6 Pinzgauer, developed by BAE Systems for the British Army. It was part of an Urgent Operational Requirement (UOR) in 2006 to provide better-protected patrol vehicles for troops operating in Afghanistan. An initial batch of 62 vehicles was delivered in 2006, followed by a further 118 examples in 2007. The majority of these were configured as troop carriers, although a small number of ambulance versions were also produced. The Vector was built on the proven chassis of the Pinzgauer 718 and was designed to offer improved mobility and protection over the Snatch Land Rover. The protection was mainly made up of Kevlar panels, including the provision of an armoured floor. This was proofed against small arms fire and shell fragments but less effective against blast. In Afghanistan, the vehicle was additionally fitted with ECM equipment to counter the increasing use of IEDs. Powered by a 109hp turbo-diesel engine, the Vector was fitted with traction control and run-flat tyres. In addition to the two-man crew, it could carry four fully equipped troops, who were provided with blast attenuating seating. Access to the rear passenger compartment was via a pair of armoured doors, although roof hatches were also fitted. Armament for local defence was normally provided by one or two roof-mounted 7.62mm GPMGs. The use of the Pinzgauer chassis and power plant allowed for useful parts commonality. However, the Vector did not prove a great success in actual use. The levels of protection it provided were simply still too inadequate to counter the increasingly powerful IEDs fielded by the Taliban. The additional weight of all the armour also led to reliability issues. This meant it was soon withdrawn from front-line service to be replaced by better-armoured types of patrol vehicles.

Vector Specifications	
Model	Vector PPV
Manufacturer	BAE Systems
Country	UK
Year	2007
Engine	VW 5-cylinder
Fuel	Diesel
Transmission	4-speed auto
Suspension	6x6
Top Speed	65mph
Range	700 miles
Armament	7.62 GPMG
Crew Capacity	2+4
Weight	4.4 tons

This three-quarter-length view gives a good impression of the 6x6 Vector. Note the front screen in a lowered position and the body covered in desert camouflage net.

Above left: A rear view showing the troop doors and roof-mounted weapon mount for a 7.62mm GPMG.

Above right: A Vector is about to go on patrol. The front screen is dropped to aid visibility and a towing strop is already attached, a wise precaution given the vehicle's reliability issues.

Below left: A rear view with the troop doors closed. Note the NATO towing hitch and steel mesh covers for the lights.

Below right: A front view displaying the slatted grill. Note the front towing pintle and wire cutter.

UK Vehicles

A Vector parked up in one of the FOBs. Note the triple windscreen wipers and desert camouflage covering the body.

This shot of a Vector and a crewman gives a good impression of the size of the vehicle. Note the warning sign on the front grill.

The Jackal MWMIK

The WMIK Land Rovers had performed well in Iraq, but the deployment into Afghanistan's wild and remote Helmand Province was to test them to the limit. With their narrow tyres, they struggled to cope with the tough terrain, while extended patrols required greater storage capacity than the 110in wheelbase could offer. The mine strikes and the Taliban's increasing use of IEDs only highlighted their vulnerability. All this experience indicated there was an urgent requirement for a vehicle with greater range, cross-country mobility and survivability than the then-current Land Rover WMIK. This is where Plymouth-based manufacturer Supacat came in, with its High Mobilty Transporter (HMT) 400, which became the Jackal in British service.

The Jackal, or Mobility Weapons Mounted Installation Kit (MWMIK) to give it its full title, came into being to fill the army's need for a new light patrol vehicle. Designed by Supacat Ltd at its Devon facility at Honiton, it was based on the HTM 400 high-mobility 4x4 platform and fitted with a powerful Cummins 5.9-litre diesel engine. Adjustable air suspension enabled a variable ride height, allowing the suspension to be raised for increased ground clearance or lowered to provide a stable firing platform. A ballistic armour package and blast attenuating crew seating afforded greater protection from IEDs, although it lacked the V-shaped hull of a fully mine-protected vehicle, like the Mastiff. Along with greater payload, protection and mobility, the Jackal featured an impressive operating range of up to 800km due to its increased fuel load. The gun ring integrated into the Roll Over Protection's (ROP) cage gave a full 360-degree traverse and enabled the mounting of a variety of weapon systems. The vehicle was also air-portable either by Chinook helicopter or RAF transport aircraft, so it could be rapidly deployed into theatre. Impressed by the new design, in 2008, the Ministry of Defence (MOD) quickly ordered 100 of the new vehicles for use in Afghanistan, where the British Army was fighting an increasingly bitter campaign against the resurgent Taliban.

First deployed into Helmand Province in 2008, it soon found itself on the front line in the hands of the parachute battalions of 16 Air Assault Brigade and Pathfinders of the Brigade Reconnaissance Force. Initially, the Jackal simply supplemented the WMIK Land Rovers, but as more became available, they became the vehicle of choice for patrolling the backcountry of Helmand. The additional range and payload it offered came into its own here, especially for extended missions mounted by the Pathfinders. With a crew of three and mounting either a .5 HMG or HK 40mm GMG, supplemented by the commander's 7.62mm GPMG, it packed a powerful punch for encounters with the Taliban. A four-vehicle callsign boasted six belt-fed machine guns, two of which were .5 calibre HMGs. This firepower was supplemented by two automatic grenade launchers, and an additional 51mm mortar was often carried by one or more vehicles. While far from being invulnerable, the Jackal did offer greater protection from the increasing IED threat and relied on its firepower, speed and mobility to get out of trouble. It quickly became a mainstay of the Brigade's operations, both as a patrol vehicle and in the fire support role. The Pathfinders ranged deep into the Afghan hinterland with their Jackals. However, it was in day-to-day patrolling and escort duties that the vehicles were mostly employed. Judged a success in this role, further batches were soon delivered, but field experience soon led to calls for improvements and modifications to the original design. Driven by operational necessity, this led directly to the rapid development of the Jackal 2.

Jackal 2 and 2A
The product improved Jackal 2 was fitted with an uprated chassis and more powerful 6.7-litre Cummins engine, allowing for a larger payload and the fitting of additional armour. This included composite side plates to protect the crew from small arms fire. The main weapon mount was moved forward, thereby improving the arc of fire. The greater load capacity of the new version meant it could now carry a four-man crew, and the MOD made an initial order for some 110 examples. These improved vehicles were first fielded in Afghanistan in 2009 and were an immediate success. Subsequently, further orders were made for 140 Jackal 2As, which featured enhanced blast protection, and these arrived in theatre from 2010 onwards. The Jackal's impressive cross-country mobility, firepower and load capacity make it an ideal choice for light reconnaissance and fire support roles. However, it is not without its faults, as the open top configuration means its crew are more exposed to small arms fire. The lack of a V-shaped hull also limits blast protection, but all military vehicle designs involve some degree of compromise. The air suspension improves on-road handling, and the variable ride height is a boon in the rough stuff. Speed and manoeuvrability offset the lack of protection, while its strategic mobility means it can be rapidly deployed to trouble spots. Developed to fill an urgent operational requirement in Afghanistan, it still finds a place in our current armed forces today.

Jackal 1 Specifications

Model	Wheeled Reconnaissance Vehicle
Manufacturer	Supacat Ltd
Country	UK
Engine	Cummins 6-cylinder 5.9-litre turbo diesel
Transmission	Allison 5-speed automatic
Suspension	Independent air springs equipped with variable ride height and run-flat tyres
Weight	6.5 tons
Range	800km (497 miles)
Road Speed	81mph
Crew Capacity	3
Armament	.50 Browning HMG or 40mm HK GMG, supplemented by commander's 7.62mm GPMG
Armour	Add-on composite armour kit
Air-portable	Chinook and Hercules/A400 Tactical Airlifter
Service Use	Now replaced by Jackal 2/2A

Jackal 2/2a Specifications

Engine	Cummins 6.7-litre turbo diesel
Transmission/ Suspension	As per the original model
Chassis	Improved over Jackal 1 with greater payload
Crew Capacity	3+1
Armament	As for Jackal 1
Armour	Enhanced underbody blast protection plus composite side armour plates. Note: Blast protection is improved with the 2a model.
Service Use	In service

The Jackal replaced the WMIK in front-line service due to its greater range payload and cross-country performance.

Above: This Jackal, pictured at one of the FOBs, displays the front-mounted smoke dischargers. A sand track and recovery strop have also been fitted and are ready for use.

Left: The driving position of the Jackal. Note the digital display and toggle-type switches.

A pair of Jackals about to go on patrol. The lead vehicle is armed with an HK 40mm GMG, while its partner mounts a .5 M2 Browning.

Above left: The commander's position with the forward mount for the 7.62mm GPMG.

Above right: This shot displays the rear deck, with its stowage bin and rear-facing smoke dischargers. Note the pioneer tools strapped to the back.

Below: A side view showing the arrangement for mounting the spare wheel and the central position of the weapon mount.

Above left: The Jackal had good underbelly protection but was far from invulnerable to IEDs.

Above right: Paratroopers fill up their Jackal with fuel at a FOB in Helmand.

Left: A Convoy of Jackals patrol an urban area in Helmand; the risk of exposure of the crew to small arms fire is clear from this image. (16 Air Assault Brigade)

Below: A Jackal 2 pictured on an exercise in the UK. This model featured improved ballistic protection and a greater payload. Note the jerrycan stowage on the rear deck.

Foxhound PPV

As mentioned, the insurgency in Iraq brutally exposed the vulnerability of the Snatch Land Rover to powerful roadside bombs and IEDs. This led to a frantic search for a replacement capable of protecting front-line troops. What was needed was a small patrol vehicle that combined the mobility of the Land Rover with the mine protection of the heavier Mastiff then coming into service. One answer turned out to be a design conceived by a British team working at Force Protection Europe. Already responsible for the heavier Mastiff series, the team's brief this time was to produce a smaller and lighter patrol vehicle with good manoeuvrability and enhanced blast protection. Working alongside F1 Engineering specialists Ricardo for the MOD's LPPV programme, the company rapidly produced a working prototype codenamed Ocelot. Two prototypes were purchased for testing purposes in April of 2010, and, by September of that year, the vehicle had been accepted under the British Army designation of Foxhound. An initial £180m order was placed for 200 vehicles as part of an UOR. This must be some kind of record within MOD procurement of an armoured vehicle, as it went from design to delivery within two years. It can also be classed as a British success story, with the rapid engineering solutions required in motorsport being applied to a defence project.

The vehicle features a full-length V-shaped mine-protected hull inspired by earlier Rhodesian and South African designs. The challenge was to fit all the automotive components, including the powerplant, fuel tank and batteries, within the armoured hull or 'skateboard'. Power came from a Styre 3.21 turbo diesel engine driving through a 6-speed ZF transmission, making the vehicle both fast and manoeuvrable. This was further enhanced by four-wheel steering, and tyre pressures could be adjusted from the cab to suit the terrain. Designed to carry a two-man crew plus four dismounts, the driving compartment is further separated from the passenger area by a bulkhead and also from the running gear, which may be affected by blast. The modular design means that any blast-damaged components can also be easily and quickly replaced in the field. The modular theme extends to the various mission-specific pods that are easily interchangeable and bolt onto the composite armoured hull. These include ambulance and logistics versions in addition to the standard PPV platform. Commanders, therefore, have the flexibility to rapidly reconfigure the vehicle by swapping the pods, and this can be achieved within 30 minutes. The initial versions went to Afghanistan for evaluation, as the Iraq mission was drawing down in 2012. Here, the vehicle quickly displayed its usefulness in the harsh conditions of Helmand although 50-degree summer temperatures did lead to some overheating problems with the engine. Despite this, Foxhound has been a success and, in the closing stages of the commitment to Afghanistan, was utilised on Force Protection duties in Kabul. The Foxhound was central to fulfilling the mission in Afghanistan, and the British Army now has a cutting-edge PPV that can get the job done while providing high levels of protection to the troops.

Foxhound Specifications	
Model	Ocelot/Foxhound PPV
Manufacturer	Force Protection Europe/Ricardo
Country	UK
Year	2010
Engine	Styre 3.21 6-cylinder 210bhp
Fuel	Diesel
Transmission	ZF 6HP28X 6-speed automatic
Suspension	4x4
Top Speed	82mph
Armament	7.62 GPMG
Crew Capacity	2+4 dismounts
Weight	7.4 tons

The Foxhound's driving position. Note the multiple switches and digital displays. (British MOD, Open Government Licence)

The new Foxhound is shown to the press during 2 Paras training for a Force Protection role in Kabul. (British MOD, Open Government Licence)

The cramped rear compartment can accommodate four dismounts on blast-attenuating seating. (British MOD, Open Government Licence)

Above: Foxhounds pictured during a pre-deployment training exercise in Stanford, UK. Note the A-frame tow bar pre-fitted to the left-hand vehicle. (British MOD, Open Government Licence)

Right: The internal arrangement of the rear cabin; even with the seats folded up, space is at a premium. (British MOD, Open Government Licence)

Below: A Foxhound on Force Protection duties in Kabul. The vehicle has retained a place in the inventory post the Afghanistan commitment. (British MOD, Open Government Licence)

Jackal and Foxhound find a continuing role with British Forces

The 20-year campaign in Afghanistan witnessed the British Army adopting a number of specialist vehicle types to contend with the tough operational conditions encountered in Helmand. These same operational imperatives led to the emergence of completely new designs, such as Jackal and Foxhound. Since the end of combat operations in 2014, much of the Afghan fleet has been withdrawn from front-line service. These specialist vehicles are now deemed unsuitable for the army's current needs and some 750 are being sold off to foreign buyers. It is therefore ironic that the two designs specifically built for Afghan conditions have gone on to find a more permanent place in the military's inventory. However, both have been put to good use in other locales. Jackals have recently been seen employed on exercises held in Poland and the Baltic states. Further afield, the Light Dragoons and Royal Anglians have taken their Jackals to Mali in support of the NATO mission. The Jackal has proved capable enough to meet the army's present operational requirements and looks set for a continuing career with UK forces. The Foxhound was also recently deployed on the UN mission to Mali. Given the increased threat levels posed by legacy mines and IEDs in many conflict zones, the Foxhound provides UK forces with a ready-made solution.

A Jackal 2 on exercise in Poland with The Queen's Dragoon Guards. (Spc Alan Prince, Public domain, via Wikimedia Commons)

A Foxhound is seen here supporting British troops on exercise in Poland. (Corporal Ben Beale, OGL v1.0OGL v1.0, via Wikimedia Commons)

EV and Hybrid Trials

Modified Jackal EVs have already been employed as trials vehicles, and both Jackals and Foxhounds are shortly to be utilised as testbeds for the latest hybrid technology. These trials are being conducted with the assistance of NP Aerospace, General Dynamics UK, Supacat and Magtec. The modified vehicles offer several tactical advantages including the ability to move silently when stealth is required. Increased electrical power is also available to run both onboard systems and external equipment. Perhaps the most useful feature might prove to be the extended range offered by hybrid propulsion systems. This new technology is being trialled under the British Army's Protected Mobility Engineering and Technical Support (PMETS) programme. The aim is to decrease the military's reliance on fossil fuels and, if successful, could be rolled out across the fleet.

The Mastiff PPV

As the British Army continued to struggle with IEDs and the issues with the Snatch Land Rover, the Americans were fairing little better with their Humvees. The challenging situation on the ground led to UORs being sent out for better-protected vehicles to counter the threat. As it happened, a small British-led team had been working on a solution at Force Protection, Inc. in the US. Using mine-protected vehicles employed in South Africa and Rhodesia as a starting point and working to a US Marine Corps (USMC) requirement, the team came up with a completely new design, named the Cougar. This came in both 4x4 and 6x6 configurations, and initial trials by the Americans proved successful, leading to some 4,000 examples being fielded by the US Army and Marine Corps. This did not go unnoticed by the British, who quickly ordered their own versions for use in Iraq and Afghanistan, conversion work being carried out by NP Aerospace. The 4x4 was named Ridgeback in British service, but it's the 6x6 version, designated Mastiff, that we are concerned with here.

The Mastiff PPV was first fielded in Afghanistan late in 2006 and featured British integrated electronics, Bowman radio fit and a slab-sided armour package. Able to carry eight fully equipped infantrymen in addition to its two-man crew and mount a selection of weaponry for local defence, it was an immediate success. This quickly led to additional purchases in 2007, followed by the development of an enhanced version. The Mastiff 2 incorporated several improvements to the design, including the use of Dyneema Unidirectional (UD) Armour. Stronger axles and suspension were also fitted to cope with the tough Afghan terrain. The turret now featured powered traverse for the gunner, and fire suppression systems were fitted to the engine and fuel tanks. The driver wasn't forgotten and gained a new thermal imager to aid situational awareness. Although the same V-shaped hull was employed along with blast-attenuating seating, overall protection was improved in the new version. As well as the troop carriers, Mastiffs were employed by the Royal Engineer IED teams and a special mine clearance version was developed. They were also used as command vehicles and armoured ambulances, while the RAF Regiment fielded the Praetorian, a version fitted with a camera system mounted on a telescopic mast. There was also a dedicated logistic version, the Wolfhound, which was used mainly for convoy work and as artillery tractors for the 105 Light Gun.

Post-Afghanistan, the design underwent additional improvements, with Mastiff 3 trials being carried out using the vehicle in a conventional mechanised infantry role. It was further proposed that Protected Mobility Battalions be equipped with the Mastiff when formed. This was something of a departure for a vehicle originally designed for counterinsurgency work. In the end, however, it was decided the Mastiff would not in fact have a future role within the British Army. Like many of the other specialist types developed for Afghanistan, the vehicles were put up for foreign sales, and, in 2022, a number have been gifted to Ukraine as part of the military support package.

Mastiff 2 Specifications	
Model	Mastiff 2 PPV
Manufacturer	Force Protection, Inc. (and NP Aerospace in Coventry for UK modifications)
Country	UK
Year	2009
Engine	Caterpillar C7 330shp
Fuel	Diesel
Range	700 miles
Transmission	Allison 3500SP automatic
Suspension	6x6
Top Speed	55mph
Armament	7.62 GPMG, .5 HMG, 40mm H&K GMG
Crew Capacity	2+8 dismounts
Weight	28 tons

Above: Although well protected, the Mastiff could still be badly damaged by IED blasts. However, the modular construction meant it could be quickly repaired.

Left: Mastiffs equipped with additional slat armour lined up at a forward base. Note the pre-fitted tow rope and camouflage netting.

Above left: Despite the size of the vehicle, the interior was quite cramped. Note the radio equipment and circular hatch for the gunner.

Above right: A rear-mounted TV screen afforded an outside view given the lack of windows.

Right: This shot, taken at one of the FOBs, gives a good impression of the size of the vehicle. Note the top-mounted exhaust system.

Below: The Mastiff's slab-sided design is clear in this shot. Note the mascot tied to the wire cutter on this 4th Battalion Royal Regiment of Scotland vehicle.

Above: The 12.7mm M2 Browning HMG was the standard armament, with the HK 40mm GMG being the alternative. Note the 'lamp-shade' ECM antenna.

Left: The front view displays the prominent slatted grill and towing eye. Note the numerous antennas for communications and ECM equipment.

Below: Troops about to en-bus via the rear armoured door. The rear-facing camera in its protective housing can be seen immediately above the opening.

Ridgback PPV

The Ridgback is the 4x4 version of the Force Protection-designed Cougar and shares many design features with the larger 6x6 Mastiff. The Cougars were ordered by the MOD in 2008 as part of an UOR, with some 150 examples being acquired. These were then further upgraded for service in Afghanistan, with the resulting vehicle named Ridgback. The enhancements included a British-designed armour package plus full radio and ECM fit. The Ridgback, therefore, offers similar protection levels to the Mastiff but in a smaller package. This means it is more suitable for operating in urban areas, where access is often restricted. Like its larger brother, this vehicle is powered by a Caterpillar C-7 330hp turbo-diesel engine driving through an Allison auto transmission. This means it enjoys a high degree of parts commonality with the Mastiff, making for easier maintenance. The Ridgback was produced in four different variants: troop carrier, fire support, ambulance and command post. It can be fitted with various armaments in a roof-mounted cupola. These include a 7.62mm GPMG, 40mm Grenade Launcher and 12.7mm HMG, and it is also possible to fit a remote weapons station. The vehicle can normally carry two crew plus six dismounts in blast-protected seating, although some versions can carry more. The Ridgback was employed in much the same role as the Foxhound, although it had a larger payload and was not quite as agile. Like many of the specialist types purchased for use in Afghanistan, the Ridgback has been earmarked to be sold off, although some will doubtless make their way to Ukraine in the form of military assistance.

Ridgback Specifications	
Model	Ridgback PPV
Manufacturer	Force Protection
Country	UK
Year	2010
Engine	Caterpillar C7 330shp
Fuel	Diesel
Range	700 miles
Transmission	Allison 3500SP automatic
Suspension	4x4
Top Speed	55mph
Armament	7.62 GPMG, .5 HMG, 40mm H&K GMG
Weight	16.9 tons

A Ridgback pictured on a winter exercise in the UK. Note the all-enveloping slat-armour and armoured turret. (British MOD, Open Government Licence)

The Ridgback is 2m shorter than the Mastiff but shares many similarities, including the V-shaped hull for blast protection. (British MOD, Open Government Licence)

Left: Though not as agile as the smaller Foxhound, the Ridgback has good cross-country mobility and is well protected. (British MOD, Open Government Licence)

Below: A Mastiff and a pair of Ridgbacks act as convoy escorts for one of the Combat Logistic Patrols (CLPs). (British MOD, Open Government Licence)

Tactical Support Vehicles (TSVs)

Yamaha Grizzly Quad Bike

Visit any military training area in the UK and you will doubtless spy a local farmer astride his quad bike, sheepdog perched on the rear deck. So it is a mystery why it took the army so long to recognise the usefulness of these little machines. In fact, it took the conflict in Afghanistan to really bring them to the fore. In Helmand, the close country of the Green Zone (bordering the Helmand River) was the focus for much of the actual fighting. The quads proved to be one of the few wheeled vehicles that could access this maze of dykes and ditches. With troops in contact, casualty evacuation could quickly become a nightmare, with long carries to a suitable helicopter landing zone (LZ). A quad and its trailer could prove vital in such circumstances, rapidly extracting a casualty and saving precious time. They were equally useful as general load luggers and became a fixture at the FOBs for recovering helicopter loads. The quads also enabled longer-duration patrols, as the accompanying trailer could carry essential supplies of water and ammunition as well as heavy weapons such as mortars. The initial purchase of quad bikes had been of stock Honda and Yamaha petrol machines, but a change was soon made to diesel versions that could run off the universal JP8 fuel. The army settled on the Yamaha Grizzly 450 Independent Rear Suspension (IRS), with infrared (IR) lighting, a winch and NATO towing eye. In 2009, the Grizzlies were uprated, the enhanced machines featuring dual throttles and double stretcher fittings for the trailers. By 2015, there were some 900 quad bikes in service, and since the end of the campaign, the quads have been retained and further upgraded, reaffirming their usefulness.

Grizzly Quad Bike Specifications	
Model	Grizzly 450 IRS
Manufacturer	Yamaha
Country	UK
Year	2003
Engine	450cc
Fuel	Diesel or JP8
Range	N/A
Transmission	Auto, selectable 2- and 4-wheel drive
Suspension	Independent front and rear
Top Speed	46mph
Armament	Personal weapons
Crew Capacity	2
Weight	281kg

A Grizzly Quad Bike at speed in Helmand. Note the 7.62mm ammunition boxes stowed up front, and the stretcher and infantry ladder on the trailer.

Above left: The Quad was one of the few wheeled vehicles that could access the narrow tracks and dykes of the Green Zone.

Above right: This shot of a Quad driver shows a typical arrangement of a liner of 7.62mm ammunition on the front stowage bin.

Below: A Quad passes a couple of locals in Helmand; these diminutive little vehicles could carry a surprising amount of kit.

Above left: A pair of Quads waiting to pick up heli-lifted stores. They could also extend the duration of foot patrols by carrying extra water and ammunition.

Above left: A heavily loaded Quad and trailer reverse onto a CH-47 Chinook before being heli-inserted into an operation.

Right: An upgraded Quad and trailer pictured during an exercise in the UK. The vehicle has been retained post-Afghanistan, having proven its usefulness.

A Quad supports a foot patrol in a rural village in Helmand. Note the driver's SA80 up front and the infantry ladders strapped to the trailer sides. (16 Air Assault Brigade)

Husky TSV

Manufactured by Navistar Defence, the Husky is a medium-armoured high-mobility TSV based on the International MXT model. The vehicle was designed specifically for the British Army in 2009, with 262 units initially ordered in 2010, followed by a further tranche of 89 machines for deployment to Afghanistan. The Husky is a four-wheel-drive medium-platform TSV designed for maximum mobility and protection. The vehicle can accommodate a four-man crew, including the driver and commander. The Husky was designed to support patrols operating in lower-threat areas and was produced in three variants. These were utility, ambulance and command post vehicles, and there was also a heavy recovery version. The utility variant is equipped with a flatbed, while the command and ambulance variations have enclosed cabs at the rear. An ambulance developed with enhanced protection entered service in 2010, along with the command post vehicle. The vehicle features a GPMG for local protection, while a remote weapon station can be fitted, capable of mounting a 12.7mm HMG. The armoured hull is designed for blast protection and can be up-armoured with either an A- or B-type appliqué armour kit. The Husky is powered by MaxxForce D6.0L V8, which provides 340bhp and drives through an Allison auto-transmission. There is a central tyre inflation system operated from the cab, and the vehicle has a maximum road speed of 70mph.

Husky Specifications	
Model	Husky TSV
Manufacturer	Navistar Defence
Country	UK
Year	2010
Engine	MaxxForce D6.0L V8
Fuel	Diesel
Transmission	Allison 2500 SP automatic
Suspension	4x4
Top Speed	70mph
Range	400 miles
Armament	7.62 GPMG or 12.7 HMG
Crew Capacity	4
Weight	6.8 tons

Opposite: A Husky TSV on patrol in Helmand. The vehicle's small footprint made it ideal for use in an urban environment. (British MOD, Open Government Licence)

Right: A Husky kicks up the dust in Helmand. Note the lamp-shaped antenna for the ECM equipment. (British MOD, Open Government Licence)

Below: This Husky, during an exercise in the UK, displays the armoured turret to good effect; this was normally fitted with a 7.62mm GPMG. (British MOD, Open Government Licence)

Above: This view shows the rear load area and armoured crew doors. Note the sand track and recovery strops. (British MOD, Open Government Licence)

Left: The Husky is based on the International MXT MRAP, as proposed for the US MRAP programme. (British MOD, Open Government Licence)

This Husky TSV is displayed at an equipment exhibition in the UK. (British MOD, Open Government Licence)

This shot of a Husky on a pre-deployment exercise in the UK gives a good impression of the size of the vehicle. Note the prominent recovery points and underbody protection. (British MOD, Open Government Licence)

Coyote TSV

Operational experience with the original Jackal highlighted the need for a support variant to improve endurance when mounting long-range patrols. Thus, the concept of the Tactical Support Vehicle (TSV) was born. Supacat based the Coyote TSV design on its HMT 600 6x6 chassis to produce a larger version of the Jackal 2. The 6x6 configuration allowed for a larger payload of up to 1.5 tonnes, while providing similar cross-country mobility to the original vehicle. Carrying a four-man crew and featuring a gun-ring plus a large flexible load space at the rear, the new vehicle was designated as the Coyote. Produced on the same Devonport production line as the Jackal 2, it featured the same enhanced armour and blast protection. An initial order of 70 vehicles was soon placed in 2009, and they began arriving in Afghanistan later that year. The Coyote was an operational success and remains in service with the army reconnaissance units that operate the Jackal 2 MWMIK.

Coyote Specifications	
Model	HMT 600
Suspension	6x6
Crew Capacity	4
Payload	1.5 tonnes with a flexible load area
Armament	Main weapon ring mount plus commander's GPMG
Armour	Blast protection as for Jackal 2
Note	Chassis lengthened over 4x4 version, while the engine and transmission remained the same.

The 6x6 Coyote was the Tactical Support Version of the Jackal and featured a flat load area at the rear with a payload of 1.5 tonnes. (British MOD, Open Government Licence)

Viking BVs10 ATV(P)

The Viking BVs10 was the armoured version of the famed 'BV206 Bandwagon' and was specially developed in 2006 for the Royal Marines, where it was designated the All Terrain Vehicle (Protected) (ATV(P)). Thirty-three of these all-terrain vehicles were initially deployed to Helmand with the Royal Marines in 2006, and they proved a great success owing to their exceptional cross-country ability. Although very similar to the Hagglunds BV206 with the same articulated dual-cab configuration, the BVs10 was a larger vehicle built on a newly developed chassis. The weight of the armoured body required a more powerful power train, and the vehicle was fitted with a Cummins 5.6-litre diesel engine. The examples used in Afghanistan were fitted with additional bar and underbelly armour, although this added two tons to the all-up weight, pushing the design close to its limits. The low ground pressure exerted by the wide tracks meant it would not trigger land mines, but the vehicle was still vulnerable to IEDs. Despite this, the Vikings proved a useful addition to the fleet, and the army asked for a permanent Viking presence to support operations. The Viking was available in several variants, including the basic troop carrier, plus command, recovery and ambulance versions. The Troop Carrier Variant (TCV) had a two-man crew and could carry up to ten passengers. The rear cab of the recovery version mounts a HIAB crane, and the Marines also used a mortar variant. The vehicle could additionally be used to carry stores and had a useful 5-ton payload. A top cover hatch was provided in the front cab for the commander, and armament options included a 7.62mm GPMG, 12.7mm HMG or 40mm GMG. Fully amphibious with minimal preparation, and still in operation today, the Viking is air portable via RAF transport aircraft and can be heli-lifted in two parts by Chinook.

This Viking, pictured in the UK, gives a good impression of the vehicle. Note the armoured windows in the turret. (British MOD, Open Government Licence)

Viking ATV(P) Specifications	
Model	BVs10
Manufacturer	Hagglunds
Country	UK
Year	2003
Engine	Cummins 5.6 litre
Fuel	Diesel
Range	300km
Transmission	Automatic
Suspension	Fully independent
Top Speed	40mph
Armament	7.62mm GPMG, 12.7 HMG or 40mm GMG
Crew Capacity	2+10 (TCV version)
Weight	10.6 tons

This rear view shows the wrap-around slat armour to good effect. Note the roof-mounted stowage bins. (British MOD, Open Government Licence)

This Viking is undergoing tests in the UK. Note the double crew doors and front-mounted grenade dischargers. (British MOD, Open Government Licence)

Top left: This shot shows the turret arrangement, mounting a 7.62mm GPMG. (British MOD, Open Government Licence)

Top right: A Viking at speed. The vehicle boasts good cross-country mobility but is lacking when it came to sufficient payload and protection levels. (British MOD, Open Government Licence)

Above: A Viking on patrol in Helmand. Its initial success led to the army requesting a permanent presence of these all-terrain vehicles. (British MOD, Open Government Licence)

Left: A Viking on operations in Helmand in 2006. Note the field-modified wire cutter fitting and the missing gun turret. (British MOD, Open Government Licence)

A convoy of Vikings during pre-deployment training in the UK. (British MOD, Open Government Licence)

Right: A well-used Viking in the Southern Desert. This vehicle has been up-gunned with a 12.7mm M2 Browning HMG. (British MOD, Open Government Licence)

Below: A Viking kicks up the dust in Helmand. (British MOD, Open Government Licence)

Warthog ATV(P)

The Warthog is based on the Bronco all-terrain tracked carrier developed by ST Kinetics for the Singapore Armed Forces. In 2008, the MOD ordered over a hundred of these vehicles as part of an UOR to replace the Vikings. This was because the Bronco offered greater protection from the increasing IED threat experienced in Afghanistan. In addition to increased survivability, the Bronco offered a larger payload than the Viking. In the British Warthog version, the vehicles were fitted with theatre-specific equipment including additional armour, specialist ECM and Bowman communication gear. Thales (UK) undertook the work to fit the additional equipment, and the vehicles began arriving in Afghanistan in 2010. Like the Viking, the Warthog runs on rubber tracks, exerting a low ground pressure and has very good cross-country performance. Power is provided by a Caterpillar C7 engine generating 350bhp, and driving is done via an Allison MD 3500 fully automatic transmission. There were four Warthog variants: troop carrier, command and control, ambulance and recovery. The troop carrier has a two-man crew and can accommodate ten dismounts, while the ambulance version carries four stretchers and has air conditioning in the rear compartment. The recovery version features a 6m crane, winch, electric generator and compressor, along with field workshop facilities.

Warthog Specifications	
Model	ATV(P)
Manufacturer	ST Kinetics
Country	UK
Year	2010
Engine	Caterpillar C7 7.2 litre 350hp
Fuel	Diesel
Transmission	Allison MD 3500 automatic
Suspension	Rubber tracked
Top Speed	60kph
Armament	7.62mm GPMG or 12.7mm HMG
Crew Capacity	2+10 dismounts
Weight	15.7 tons

The Warthog during testing in the UK. Note the forward-mounted grenade dischargers and prominent armoured turret. (British MOD, Open Government Licence)

Above: A general view of the vehicle with its twin cabs and rubber tracks, which are very similar to the Hagglunds Viking. (British MOD, Open Government Licence)

Right: A Warthog at speed in Helmand, where its impressive cross-country performance came to the fore. (British MOD, Open Government Licence)

Below: A convoy of Warthogs in Helmand. Note the slat armour and numerous antennas for communications and ECM gear. (British MOD, Open Government Licence)

A Warthog displays its amphibious capability while crossing a river in Afghanistan. (British MOD, Open Government Licence)

Left: This Warthog is pictured in the typical desert environment of southern Afghanistan. Note the jerrycans stowed on the rear cab. (British MOD, Open Government Licence)

Below left: This view gives a good impression of the slat armour fitted as protection from RPG strikes; this example is armed with a 7.62mm GPMG. (British MOD, Open Government Licence)

Below right: Crew members pose with their vehicle. The Warthog offered greater levels of protection than the Viking it replaced. (British MOD, Open Government Licence)

Specialist Vehicles

Panther CLV

In 2008, a new vehicle began field trials in Afghanistan, designed to fulfil the Command and Liaison (CLV) role: the Panther CLV. At first glance, this vehicle appeared not unlike a heavily armoured Land Rover. However, a peek inside revealed a surprisingly cramped interior packed with electronics and radio gear. The MOD first issued a requirement for a Future Command and Liaison Vehicle (FCLV) in 2001 to replace a range of types currently in service, including Land Rovers, Saxons and various Combat Vehicle Reconnaissance Tracked (CVRTs). Trails were initiated to find a suitable candidate, with several manufacturers putting forward their designs. These included the RG32M from Vickers, the ACMAT from Hunting Engineering, the IVECO Puma and an armoured Land Rover from NP Aerospace. From this selection, the RG32M appeared to be the hot favourite. However, the IVECO LMV (Light Multi-Role Vehicle) was controversially submitted at the last minute and selected instead. A contract for 401 examples of the new vehicle was awarded in 2003, with the option for further orders to follow. Series production began in 2006 under the designation of the Panther CLV. The type subsequently entered service with the British Army in 2008 and was to have a troubled history, but first let's look more closely at its design.

The Panther was based on the IVECO LMV, which was already in service with the armed forces of Italy, Belgium and Spain among others. Built with a V-shaped body for mine protection, it featured a sandwich construction for the hull floor to cushion the occupants from blast. The vehicle also came with modular ballistic armour, offering protection from small arms fire. An add-on package could be fitted to withstand munitions up to 14.5mm, plus blast and fragmentation from IEDs. Power was derived from an IVECO F1C turbo diesel, which produced 182bhp, and was driven through a six-speed automatic gearbox. For armament, a Galileo-designed Remote Control Weapon Station (RCWS) was mounted on the roof. This was designated 'Enforcer' and featured a Surveillance, Target Acquisition Weapon Sight (STAWS), which included thermal imaging. This turret could accommodate both 7.62mm and 12.7mm MGs, or alternatively a 40mm Automatic Grenade Launcher. In service, the vehicles appear to have been generally fitted with a 7.62mm GPMG, and these were controlled from the cab via a camera and joystick. Inside, the crew was provided with air conditioning and blast-attenuating seating, although internal space was very limited. A full Bowman vehicle fit plus ECM equipment occupied the rear of the cab, although this was to cause overheating problems in use. Because of this and the high IED threat in theatre, the Panther was not used operationally in Iraq. Instead, up-armoured FV432 Bulldogs mounting the same RCWS turret were employed in the role. This was somewhat embarrassing, considering the Panther was supposedly purpose-designed for the job.

As a result of these issues, a series of hot weather trials were held before the type's operational deployment, which led to several modifications to the vehicle. These included the addition of a crew roof hatch, revised engine intake, rear-view camera and additional armour protection. Some 67 vehicles were modified to this standard and deployed to Afghanistan in 2009. They were mainly used by the RAC Close Support Regiment, but more issues were soon to raise their ugly heads. Internal space was very limited once all that radio and ECM equipment was packed in, leaving little room for the crew and their personal equipment. Meanwhile, all those electronics generated a lot of excess heat, which was an issue given that outside temperatures in Helmand could reach 40 degrees plus. Then there was the extra weight of all that armour and equipment putting additional strain on the running gear and transmission. This led to breakdowns and low-availability rates, while the Panther's cross-country performance proved disappointing in Helmand's rugged backcountry. All these factors led to the vehicles spending much of their time at the field workshops in Camp Bastion. As a result, they were generally replaced by the Husky and Wolfhound, once sufficient numbers became available. Both of these latter PPVs offered a greater payload and improved mobility over the Panther, which was largely withdrawn from front-line use. A recent review concluded the CLV role would be better fulfilled by other vehicles going forward. Presumably, modified versions of the Foxhound and the new Boxer Mechanised Infantry Vehicle will take on the CLV role in the future.

Panther Specifications	
Model	Panther CLV
Manufacturer	IVECO
Country	Italy/UK BAE Systems
Year	2006
Engine	IVECO F1C 182 bhp
Fuel	Diesel
Range	310 miles
Transmission	6-speed automatic gearbox
Suspension	4x4 Independent Double A-Arm
Top Speed	80mph (road)
Armament	RCWS with 7.62mm GPMG
Crew Capacity	3
Weight	6.5 tons

The Panther CLV undergoing trials. Note the roof-mounted remote weapon station and antenna bracket. (British MOD, Open Government Licence)

The Panther is pictured at an equipment demonstration. Note the twin armoured crew doors and rear plastic tilt for the load area. (British MOD, Open Government Licence)

Right: The Vickers RG32M, which was initially the favourite to fulfil the command and liaison (CLV) role. (British MOD, Open Government Licence)

Below: This shot of a Panther CLV paired with a WMIK Land Rover gives a good impression of the vehicle's dimensions. (British MOD, Open Government Licence)

A Panther on patrol in Afghanistan accompanied by a Jackal; the Panther was to struggle in the heat and rugged terrain encountered in Helmand. (British MOD, Open Government Licence)

A Panther pictured on operations. Note the top cover hatch and stowage of the crew's bergens from the side of the load area. (British MOD, Open Government Licence)

Scimitar Mk 2

The veteran Scimitar CVRT found a new lease of life in Afghanistan and, with its potent mix of mobility and firepower, it proved a useful asset. Nevertheless, the harsh operating conditions of Helmand threw up several issues that needed addressing. The fact was, after decades of service, from the Falklands to Bosnia and Iraq, these Cold War warriors were in dire need of an upgrade to remain effective on the modern battlefield. Under an UOR, improvements were rapidly made to the engine, transmission and gearbox, while the addition of air conditioning and sand filters improved crew comfort. Also on the menu was improved communications and night-vision equipment. These enhancements all made a difference, but it was soon recognised that far more fundamental changes were required, which was to lead directly to the Scimitar Mk 2.

A contract for a modernised CVRT was awarded in December 2010, and BAE Systems quickly began development work at its Telford site. The fact that the upgraded vehicle was required for operational service in Afghanistan added extra impetus to the work. The decision was taken to base the project around a hull design based on the Spartan APC. Constructed from aluminium, it featured built-in mine-blast protection and improved armour. It also offered more space for the crew and an emergency egress route for the driver. A new engine was fitted, the Cummins BTA 5.9 diesel, which was mated to a David Brown TN15E+ automatic gearbox. This improved both the power output and reliability, while the frugality of the diesel increased range and endurance. Torsion bar suspension was still utilised, although in an enhanced version and either rubber or metal tracks could be fitted. When it came to armament, the standard Rarden 30mm was retained; originally designed back in the 1960s, it was improved in the 1980s to the current L21A1 standard. An automatic cannon loaded from three-round clips, it can be fired single shot or in bursts of up to six rounds. The Rarden has had its problems over the years, but it is accurate and generally reliable, also arming the Warrior IFV. A co-axial 7.62mm L7 GPMG was mounted to the left of the main armament and operated through a solenoid. A host of other improvements were also included in the design, such as blast-attenuating crew seating, improved air conditioning, enhanced night-vision equipment, turret roll-over protection and ECM equipment. Eventually, these improvements were to be rolled out across the CVRT family, but the first Scimitar Mk 2s began to come into service in theatre late in 2011.

The users' opinions on the new vehicle were generally favourable; especially appreciated was the larger crew compartment and enhanced blast protection. The higher silhouette brought some advantages in improved observation and target acquisition. The new turret system also offered improved stability over the older model. The rebuilt vehicles proved reliable in use and easier to maintain in the field. Serviceability is important, and poor reliability was something that had be-devilled British armour over the years. The Scimitar Mk 2 received its baptism of fire in Afghanistan and remains in service today, although the reconnaissance version of the Future Rapid Effects System SV (FRES SV) will eventually replace it. The CVRT family has been a great success story and has proved highly adaptable to changing battlefield conditions. The Spartan APC version has recently been supplied to the Ukrainians, and we are likely to see these classic Armoured Fighting Vehicles (AFVs) around for some time to come.

Scimitar Mk 2 Specifications	
Make	CVRT
Model	Scimitar Mk 2
Manufacturer	BAE Systems
Country	UK
Year	2009
Engine	Cummins BTA 5.9
Fuel	Diesel
Transmission	TN15E+ automatic gearbox
Suspension	Torsion bar
Tracks	Metal or rubber
Armament	Rarden 30mm automatic cannon; co-axial 7.62mm L7 GPMG
Weight	12 tons

A Scimitar is undergoing maintenance at a FOB in Helmand. Note the multiple antennas for communications and ECM equipment.

This shot displays the slat armour to good advantage, designed to defeat the rocket-propelled grenades (RPGs) used by the insurgents.

Left: A typical Scimitar on patrol in Helmand, with its turret reversed.

Below: This shot of the turret shows the prominent gunner's and commander's periscopes, and the multiple antennas.

A Scimitar covers a foot patrol mounted from one of the FOBs. This shot displays the rear arrangement of the slat or bar armour.

Right: Scimitars parked up at one of the FOBs. This Cold War warrior found a new lease of life in Afghanistan.

Below: A Scimitar at speed; the vehicle's impressive speed and cross-country mobility were an advantage in Helmand's rugged backcountry.

Above: Scimitar Mk 2s about to go on patrol. The vehicle's high silhouette is obvious here.

Left: The Scimitar Mk 2 utilised a new hull based on the Spartan APC; this raised the silhouette of the vehicle but allowed for more crew room. (British MOD, Open Government Licence)

M270 MLRS

The M270 MLRS is a 227mm American-designed Multiple Launch Rocket System (MLRS) manned by the Royal Artillery. This self-propelled artillery rocket system features twin rocket pods and has a range of some 30km. First going into service with the US Army in 1983, it was adopted by a number of NATO countries including the UK. It was first used operationally in the Gulf War of 1991, where it proved its effectiveness. Each disposable pod contains six rockets, which can be fired individually or as a single 'fire for effect' of 12 rockets. There is no launching rail, and the rockets are fired directly from their pods. Reloading is power-assisted and can be accomplished in 8–10 minutes by a trained crew. Before deployment to Afghanistan, the system was upgraded to the GMLRS standard (G for GPS). These updated rockets have been fitted with a guidance system using a combination of inertial navigation and jam-resistant GPS and have a range in excess of 70km. The accuracy is reportedly extremely high, with the near-vertical terminal trajectory proving extremely useful when engaging insurgents fighting from compounds. The M31A1 GMLRS rocket is fitted with a single blast warhead, and the fuse has three modes: point, delay and air-burst. A number of GMLRs were positioned on FOBs, but their use was often limited for fear of causing unintended civilian casualties. The MLRS system itself is mounted on the chassis of the US Bradley IFV, giving it good tactical mobility. The British version features an armoured cab and enhanced protection against IEDs. The destructive power of the weapon system perhaps makes it more useful in a general war scenario than in an insurgency. This has recently been illustrated with the use of the MLRS in the war in Ukraine, where it has proved highly effective.

MLRS Specifications	
Model	M270B1 (British variant)
Manufacturer	Lockheed Martin
Country	UK
Year	2003
Engine	Cummins 500hp
Fuel	Diesel
Transmission	Automatic gearbox
Suspension	Torsion bar
Range	298 miles
Top Speed	39mph
Armament	M269 Launcher Loader Module
Crew Capacity	3
Weight	24.5 tons

This shot gives a good view give of the twin pods, each containing six pre-packed rockets.

The pre-packed rocket pods can be rapidly reloaded in a matter of minutes, assisted by the vehicle's integral crane.

Left: This side view shows the add-on slat armour and illustrates the relatively small crew compartment.

Below: These patrol members walking by give a good impression of the size of the M270 MLRS (Multiple Launch Rocket System), which has quite a low silhouette.

This front view displays the slat armour and narrow armoured window slots.

Right: This three-quarter view gives a good impression of the vehicle that sits on the chassis and running gear of the Bradley IFV.

Below: This MLRS is paired with its loading vehicle, which features an integral crane. The rocket pods are raised to launch position, although they would never be fired from the base, given the considerable back blast.

Trojan ARVE

First deployed to Afghanistan in 2009, the Trojan ARVE (Armoured Recovery Vehicle Engineers) was specially designed by BAE Systems for clearing mines and manned by the Royal Engineers. Based on a modified Challenger 2 Main Battle Tank chassis, the turret was removed and replaced by a new superstructure with special engineer equipment. The Trojan is fitted with a mine plough, dozer blade and a large hydraulic excavator arm. The arm can also be used to grab and move obstacles and deposit the fascine the Trojan carries on its rear deck. Meanwhile, the full-length plough pushes mines aside to clear a safe path for following vehicles. A clear lane-marking system can also be fitted. The mine plough can be easily replaced with a dozer blade, which is used to create earthworks. The fascines are used for bridging ditches, while a towed trailer can carry the Python rocket-propelled minefield breaching system. With thousands of 'legacy mines' left behind by the Russians, the Trojan came into its own in Afghanistan and followed a long line of ARVE tanks, which began with the modified Churchills of World War Two.

Trojan Specifications	
Model	ARVE
Manufacturer	BAE Systems
Country	UK
Year	2007, first deployed 2009
Engine	Perkins CV12-8A 1200
Fuel	Diesel
Range	280 miles
Transmission	TN54ETS, 6 forward, 2 reverse gears
Suspension	Hydropneumatic
Top Speed	37mph
Armament	7.62mm GPMG
Crew Capacity	3
Weight	62.5 tons

Above left: The Trojan ARVE at work in Afghanistan, with the mine plough deployed. Note that the three crew members each have an individual hatch. (16 Air Assault Brigade)

Above right: This front view shows the mine plough in operation. Note the forward-mounted grenade dischargers. (16 Air Assault Brigade)

Above: A pair of Trojan ARVEs (Armoured Recovery Vehicle Engineers) on a clearance operation in Helmand. The high prevalence of legacy mines from the Soviet era made this work essential. (British MOD, Open Government Licence)

Right: A Trojan ARVE pictured in the UK. The dozer blade is fitted, and a fascine is carried on the rear deck. (British MOD, Open Government Licence)

A Trojan on pre-deployment training in the UK. Both the mine-plough and dozer blade are fitted, and the impressive size of the excavator's arm is worth noting. (British MOD, Open Government Licence)

Logistics Vehicles

MAN SV Truck

The 4x4 SV truck is the British Army variant of the Rheinmetall MAN HX60 Tactical Truck, of which the UK was the first user. The MAN HX was specifically designed for military use and is available in 4x4, 6x6 and 8x8 configurations. Powered by a turbocharged 326hp diesel engine driving through a 12-speed ZF auto transmission, the truck has good cross-country mobility. Additional armour can be fitted to the cab and there is a roof hatch for top cover and mounting of 7.62mm MG. The MAN SV is designed to transport troops and general cargo and in Afghanistan was primarily used as a load lugger.

MAN SV Specifications	
Model	MAN HX60 Truck
Manufacturer	Rheinmetall
Country	UK
Year	1999
Engine	MAN 326hp turbo-charged
Fuel	Diesel
Range	800km
Transmission	12-speed ZF auto
Suspension	Fully independent
Top Speed	88kph (limited)
Armament	7.62mm GPMG
Crew Capacity	2 plus
Weight	7 tons

The MAN SV was a general load lugger and was equipped with an up-armoured cab and additional slat armour for Afghanistan. (British MOD, Open Government Licence)

MAN EPLS

The Enhanced Pallet Load System or EPLS was the backbone of the British Army's logistic effort in Afghanistan. Based on the ubiquitous MAN 8x8 Truck, it featured a 15-ton flatrack payload enabling the rapid loading and unloading of ISO containers. The EPLS is a modern replacement for the older Foden Drops vehicle, which struggled to cope with the operational conditions in Afghanistan. The vehicle rapidly became a key component of the Combat Logistic Patrols (CLPs) mounted to support the FOBs. The EPLS featured a rear-mounted camera system to aid with the loading process, while the modular military spec cab featured climate control and additional ballistic protection for the crew. The MAN EPLS continues in service with the British Armed Forces and a substantial number have been updated to the EPLS Mk 3 standard. This includes a new hook loading system for flatracks produced by HIAB of Sweden.

EPLS Specifications	
Model	MAN EPLS
Manufacturer	Rheinmetall
Country	UK
Year	2008
Engine	D2066 LF34 10.5-litre turbocharged diesel
Fuel	Diesel
Range	800km
Transmission	12-speed ZF auto
Suspension	8x8 fully independent
Top Speed	88kph (limited)
Armament	7.62mm GPMG
Crew Capacity	2 plus
Weight	7 tons

A Foden Drops vehicle leads a road convoy of MAN EPLS trucks delivering supplies to the forward units. Note the EPLS features an armoured turret for the gunner. (British MOD, Open Government Licence)

The MAN EPLS featured hydraulic stabilising legs and a 15-ton flatrack for the loading of ISO containers. (British MOD, Open Government Licence)

Left: EPLS trucks on the move with their load of ISO containers. This must be a safe area as the top cover positions are unmanned. (British MOD, Open Government Licence)

Below: An EPLS pictured in the UK. Note the additional slat armour and the armoured turret for the top cover. (British MOD, Open Government Licence)

Oshkosh Fuel Tanker

The Oshkosh Fuel Tanker was specifically designed for the British MOD and was employed both in Iraq and Afghanistan. The towing unit is based on the proven 6x6 Medium Tactical Vehicle Replacement (MTVR) tractor. This is mated to the 5,280-gallon Close Support Tanker (CST). There are also tanker units available for aviation fuel (3,960 gallons) and water (4,755 gallons).

The MTVR features all-wheel drive and the TAK 4 suspension system, giving it good cross-country performance. There is also a central tyre inflation system operated from the cab, which can change the tyre pressures to suit the terrain. The bulk of the trailers procured was of the CST variant for fuel and the combination of tractor and trailer is air portable by RAF C-130 or C-17 Globemaster aircraft.

Fuel Tanker Specifications	
Model	MTVR
Manufacturer	Oshkosh
Country	UK
Year	2001
Engine	Caterpillar C-12 425hp
Fuel	Diesel
Range	483km
Transmission	auto
Suspension	TAC fully independent
Top Speed	105kph (road)
Armament	7.62mm GPMG
Crew Capacity	2
Weight	12.6 tons (tractor unit)

The Oshkosh tankers provided a vital role in supplying fuel to the forward bases in Helmand.

An Oshkosh tanker disgorges its fuel load at one of the FOBs in the Sangin valley. Driving one of these was a dangerous job given the prevalence of roadside bombs and IEDs.

Oshkosh Heavy Equipment/Tank Transporter

The Oshkosh 1070F replaced the older Scammel Commander tank transporter for the movement of heavy equipment. The standard Oshkosh 1070 model received modifications to the cab, engine and transmission to meet the British requirements. The transporter is powered by a Caterpillar C-18 six-cylinder engine turbo-diesel engine producing 700hp. The trailer unit is fitted with a twin winch and utilises a British-built Kings GTS 100 hydraulic tilting trailer. Capable of carrying all types of heavy equipment, the transporter was also used to recover vehicles damaged by IED blasts. It remains in service with the British military in its primary role as a tank transporter.

Heavy Equipment Transporter Specifications	
Model	1070F
Manufacturer	Oshkosh
Country	UK
Year	2001
Engine	Caterpillar C-18 700hp
Fuel	Diesel
Range	523 miles
Transmission	Allison HD 4076P automatic
Suspension	Parabolic leaf front plus air rear.
Top Speed	81kph (road)
Armament	7.62mm GPMG
Crew Capacity	2
Weight	N/A

The Oshkosh Heavy Equipment Transporters could be used for vehicle recovery, and several were used to transport the new turbine to Kajaki. (British MOD, Open Government Licence)

Chapter 2

US Vehicles

Light Vehicles

The Ford Ranger

With literally thousands in use by the US and Allied military, the Ford Ranger became ubiquitous in Afghanistan. Afghan security forces would routinely shuttle soldiers and police around the country in these tough pickup trucks and, post-conflict, numerous captured examples were to be seen in the hands of the Taliban. Robust and mechanically simple, they became the jack of all trades used by everyone from government agencies to Special Forces. The UK's Ricardo Engineering upgraded many of these trucks, giving them a higher ride height with improved heavy-duty suspension and long-range fuel tanks. These militarised versions came with roll-over and armour protection extra stowage and bulletproof glass for the windows. It's unclear just how many were configured to this military specification, but it must have been a substantial number as they were a common sight. The Ford Ranger is a 4x4 double cab pickup with a turbo-diesel 2.2-litre engine. It drives through a 6-speed manual transmission and sits on coil-front and leaf-rear suspension. Mechanically simple and robust, the Ranger is effectively the US equivalent of the Toyota Hilux, the favourite mount of the Taliban.

Ford Ranger Specifications	
Model	Ranger Double Cab Pickup
Manufacturer	Ford
Country	US
Year	2006
Engine	2.2-litre TDCi
Fuel	Diesel
Transmission	6-speed manual
Suspension	4x4 coil and leaf sprung
Top Speed	70mph
Armament	7.62mm M240 or PK MG
Crew Capacity	5
Weight	1.7 tons

A Ford Ranger double-cab in Afghan Police service, with a typical armament of a pintle-mounted 7.62mm PK MG. (Master Sgt Juan Valdes USAF, Public domain, via Wikimedia Commons)

Above left: A typical Ranger in Helmand – many thousands were supplied to the Afghan Security Forces in both single- and double-cab form. (David Gunn, Public domain, via Wikimedia Commons)

Above right: Taliban fighters riding in a captured police vehicle. Large numbers of these Ford pickups were left behind after the withdrawal in 2021. (Callum Darragh, CC0, via Wikimedia Commons)

Left: The Afghan Police used large numbers of Ford Rangers, a typical example of which is operating in southern Helmand. (Cpl Alex Guerra, Public domain, via Wikimedia Commons)

Below left: An Afghan Army single-cab pickup. These rugged 4x4s had good cross-country performance. (koldo hormaza from Madrid, España, CC BY-SA 2.0 https://creativecommons.org/licenses/by-sa/2.0, via Wikimedia Commons)

Below right: Rangers were also popular with US and Allied Special Forces operating in Afghanistan. (Unknown author, Public domain, via Wikimedia Commons)

Humvee M1115

The Humvee was produced by American Motors General, and the company turned to one of its subsidiaries, O'Gara-Hess & Eisenhardt, to install a suitable armour package. The Armour Survivability Kit (ASK) was rapidly developed and fitted to up-armoured Humvees. This package included 2in-thick glass for the front screen and side windows, plus a metal and Kevlar composite bulletproof skin. The underside of the vehicle was also fitted with blast plates for protection against mines and IEDs. An initial order was placed for 1,200 vehicles, and on average it would take around four days to add the armour to a standard Humvee. An improved FRAG-5 armour protection kit offered even higher levels of protection at the penalty of increased weight, and vehicles were soon being produced at the rate of 450 a month. The decision was then taken to up-armour the entire fleet deployed to Iraq, some 8,000 vehicles in total. With ever more powerful IEDs employed by the insurgents, including Explosively Formed Penetrators (EFPs), the armour package soon required a further upgrade. This FRAG-6 kit replaced the original ⅜in steel armour with ⅝in panel. The underbody protection was also improved, and ballistic glass was added to the list of protective features. Coming in at around 1,500lb, however, the extra weight of all the armour was having a detrimental effect on performance. Additional upgrades were therefore required to the suspension, along with improved cooling provided for the engine. This Level 2 FRAG-6 armour package was deemed to be the most that the chassis could reasonably take in a vehicle originally designed as a soft-skinned personnel and cargo carrier. Although the FRAG-5 and 6 protection did offer increased survivability for the crew, issues were soon discovered with the armoured doors. These could become jammed shut as the result of a blast, trapping those inside. A special D-ring was therefore rapidly supplied to enable the doors to be wrenched off in an emergency with the aid of a tow cable and a second vehicle.

Originally, the hardtop Humvees came with a ring mount fitted as standard, allowing the vehicle to be armed with a variety of weapon types. The usual armament was a Mk 19 40mm GMG or .5 Browning HMG, each attached via a pintle with 360-degree traverse. A TOW missile could also be mounted using the same system. In 2004, an adapter was made available to fit a secondary weapon such as an M249 5.56mm SAW alongside the main armament, increasing the available firepower. Early combat experience such as the fighting in Mogadishu soon exposed the vulnerability of gunners to small arms fire, and further modifications to the ring mount were made adding an armoured shield. Side and rear armoured panels were soon included in the gunner's protection package, which led to the development of a fully armoured turret. Several designs of the turret were tried before the US Army eventually settled on the Objective Gunner Protection Kit (O-GPK). This included armoured glass side windows and an optional armoured roof panel. As usual, the Marine Corps went its own way and adopted the Marine Corps Transparent Armoured Gun Shield (MCTAGS) designed by BAE Systems. A collapsible version of this turret, the MCTAGS-R, was also developed, allowing the shipping height to be reduced for amphibious operations.

The progressive improvements in the Humvees protection levels driven by operational necessity eventually led to the standardised M1151 Enhanced Armament Carrier. This was built on a new heavy-duty chassis with an uprated suspension to handle the weight of the armour. Power was provided by a GEP V8, 6.5-litre turbocharged diesel engine, providing 190hp and driving through a 4-speed auto gearbox. There were two armour packages available: the A kit installed at the factory and a bolt-on B kit to improve the protection levels where required. Run-flat tyres were fitted as standard, with a central tyre inflation system operated from the cab. There were several variants produced, including a two-door cargo carrier, the M1152, and the pickup version, the M1165. A couple of ambulance variants were also fielded capable of carrying either two or four litter cases. The M1151 was intended to replace all earlier versions of the armoured Humvee then in service. However, despite the enhanced armour protection, it still proved vulnerable to the increasingly sophisticated and powerful IEDs fielded by the insurgents. This led to the search for a specifically designed and mine-proofed vehicle, which culminated in the adoption of the Mine Resistant, Ambush Protected (MRAP) vehicles.

Over the years, literally thousands of armoured Humvees of various types were supplied to the Afghan National Army. This made sense, as they offered armoured protection and enhanced firepower to lightly armed security forces. They were also simple to maintain and operate, an important consideration for militaries lacking sophisticated technical backup. As a result, however, large numbers of Humvees were lost to the insurgents in the wake of the withdrawal from Afghanistan. In the wake of the government collapse, Taliban fighters were seen parading the streets of Kabul in these captured Humvees. Many of these vehicles were later used by the Taliban to suppress the opposition in the Panjshir Valley. Recent reports also suggest that a large number of Humvees and other US equipment have been supplied to Iran in return for oil deals. All of this means we will more than likely see armoured Humvees in the hands of insurgent groups for many years to come.

Humvee M1115 Specifications	
Type	Light Armoured Vehicle
Engine	GEP V8, 6.5-litre 190hp turbo-diesel
Transmission	4-speed automatic
Suspension	Independent 4x4 (permanent 4-wheel drive, high/low transfer box)
Armament	Mk 19 GMG or .50 HMG in armoured turret
Range	250 miles
Top road speed	70mph
Weight	3.7 tons

The result of an IED strike in Iraq, where the Humvee proved vulnerable. (Public domain, via Wikimedia Commons)

A later M1151 Humvee with enhanced armour and turret. This only proved a stopgap until the better protected Mine Resistant, Ambush Protected (MRAP) came along. (Bayshoremods, CC BY-SA 3.0 https://creativecommons.org/licenses/by-sa/3.0, via Wikimedia Commons)

Above left: The M1151 Humvee in its final form – armament would normally be something more substantial than a 5.56mm M16. (U.S. Marine Corps photo by Lance Cpl Olivia G. Ortiz/Released, Public domain, via Wikimedia Commons)

Above right: An up-armoured Humvee. Note the doors have yet to be fitted with D-rings to aid extraction. (US Navy photo by Photographer's Mate 3rd Class Shawn Hussong, Public domain, via Wikimedia Commons)

The O-GPK gave the gunner all-around protection and 360-degree traverse for the 12.7mm M2 Browning HMG. (Todd Huffman from Phoenix, AZ, CC BY 2.0 https://creativecommons.org/licenses/by/2.0, via Wikimedia Commons)

An Afghan Army Humvee. Note the box body and 7.62mm top cover armament. (Cpl Reece Lodder, Public domain, via Wikimedia Commons)

MRAPs

The MRAP Programme

The US Humvee went through a similar trial by fire as the British Snatch Land Rover in Iraq and Afghanistan, which sparked a search for a better-protected replacement. The result was the Mine Resistant, Ambush Protected (MRAP) programme to develop vehicles that could withstand the blast from insurgent IEDs. The first vehicle to emerge from the programme was the Force Protection Cougar in 2004, which was actually the brainchild of a small British design team. The vehicle featured a V-shaped hull similar to earlier Rhodesian and South African mine-resistant vehicles. The first Cougars were rushed to Afghanistan and Iraq as part of an urgent operational requirement and were an immediate success. The vehicle's proven ability to withstand IED blasts and reduce casualties led to it being chosen by the British as the basis for the Mastiff PPV. Further designs were to follow, including the International MaxxPro and Caiman. These propose-built types rapidly took over from the Humvees with their bolt-on armour packages.

The key feature of the Cougar MRAP is undoubtedly its V-shaped armoured hull, designed to deflect the blast from IEDs and mine strikes. The modular design of the suspension and running gear means the vehicle can then be rapidly put back into service. Survivability is at the heart of the design, with advanced ballistic protection for the crew and the ability of the vehicle to withstand both small arms and RPG strikes. The Cougar went into service in 2003, and since then there have been no reported crew fatalities, despite hundreds of attacks from IEDs. The Cougar MRAP was available in 4x4 and 6x6 variants, both powered by a Caterpillar C-7 diesel engine driving through a six-speed Allison automatic transmission. The 6x6 version can accommodate up to ten fully equipped troops with a two- or three-man crew. Armament consists of a roof-mounted 7.62mm M240 MG, 12.7mm Browning HMG or Mk 19 40mm Automatic Grenade Launcher. A Remote Weapon Station can also be fitted, while some versions feature firing ports in the hull. The Cougar came in different versions for specialist tasks, including a Hardened Engineer Vehicle (HEV) and the Joint Explosive Ordinance Disposal (EOD) Rapid Response Vehicle (JERRV). It was to prove invaluable for moving men and materiel to and from remote FOBs in Afghanistan.

Cougar MRAP Specifications	
Model	Force Protection Cougar
Manufacturer	General Dynamics
Country	US
Year	2003
Engine	Caterpillar C-7 330hp
Fuel	Diesel
Transmission	Allison 3500 SP automatic
Suspension	4x4 and 6x6
Top Speed	65mph
Range	420 miles
Armament	7.62 M240, 12.7 HMG or Mk 19 GMG
Crew Capacity	2+10 (6x6 version)
Weight	24.5 tons

Right: Cougar 6x6 MRAPs – these were the base vehicle for the British Mastiff. Note the distinctive side windows and armoured turret for the gunner. (US Navy photo by Mass Communication Specialist 2nd Class Dustin Coveny, Public domain, via Wikimedia Commons)

Below: The MRAPs were well protected but far from invulnerable, as illustrated by this Cougar that suffered an IED strike. The crew all survived. (US Military, Public domain, via Wikimedia Commons)

International MaxxPro MRAP

While the Cougar filled the role of an IED- and mine-protected troop carrier, there was also a requirement for a smaller MRAP for patrol and escort duties. Navistar International, therefore, developed the MaxxPro in conjunction with Israeli company Plasan. Like the Cougar, the MaxxPro features a mine-resistant V-shaped hull and ballistic armour designed by Plasan. The chassis was taken from the International WorkStar 7000 truck, and the vehicle is powered by a D9 316 diesel engine. The MaxxPro underwent testing at the US Army's Aberdeen proving ground in 2007, with deliveries starting in 2008. There are three basic versions of the MaxxPro MRAP, all of which share the same platform. These are the MaxxPro Plus, the MaxxPro Dash and the MaxxPro XL. The MaxxPro Plus features increased engine power and payload, with extra protection from shaped charge explosive penetrators. The MaxxPro Dash is a smaller variant with greater mobility, designed to be less prone to roll-over – a common problem with MRAPs, owing to the high ground clearance and weight of armour. Finally, the MaxxPro XL is a larger Category 2 vehicle featuring a longer wheelbase that can carry up to ten dismounts. There are also ambulance, recovery and command post variants of the vehicle. In Afghanistan, the MaxxPro gradually took over from the armoured Humvee in front-line use.

MaxxPro Specifications	
Model	MaxxPro MRAP
Manufacturer	Navistar International
Country	US
Year	2007
Engine	MaxxForce D9.316 330hp, (375hp in later versions)
Fuel	Diesel
Transmission	Allison 3000 5-speed automatic
Suspension	4x4 semi-elliptical leaf-sprung
Top Speed	65mph
Range	370 miles
Armament	7.62 M240, 12.7 HMG or Mk 19 GMG
Crew Capacity	3+7 (+10 for the XL version)
Weight	12.7 tons (13.4 for XL)

This shot of the MaxxPro MRAP gives a good impression of the height and size of the vehicle. The O-GPK armoured turret was originally developed for the Humvee. (https://www.flickr.com/photos/mallard10/3364731344, CC BY 2.0 https://creativecommons.org/licenses/by/2.0, via Wikimedia Commons)

A line-up of MaxxPro MRAPs pictured at a FOB in Afghanistan. These examples are in Romanian service. (Radu Mureșan, CC BY-SA 3.0 https://creativecommons.org/licenses/by-sa/3.0, via Wikimedia Commons)

MaxxPro MRAPs on patrol in Afghanistan. Note the additional slat armour and O-GPK turrets with sunshades. (Spc Austin Berner, Public domain, via Wikimedia Commons)

The Oshkosh M-ATV was designed to be more manoeuvrable in Afghanistan's rugged terrain and is pictured here with the larger MaxxPro MRAP. (Spc Elisebet Freeburg, Joint Sustainment Command-Afghanistan PAO, Public domain, via Wikimedia Commons)

Caiman MRAP

The Caiman was developed by Armour Holdings and BAE Systems on the chassis and running gear of the Medium Tactical Vehicle (MTV) series of US tactical trucks. This made for useful parts commonality and kept development costs down. Selected by the US Marine Corps, it came in both 4x4 and 6x6 versions as Category 1 and 2 MRAPs. In common with other mine-resistant designs, it features a V-shaped hull, but this does not extend to the engine compartment. The crew are further protected by a monolithic floor, blast-attenuating seats and an automatic fire suppression system. The armour provides protection against IEDs, mines, RPG rounds and small arms fire. The Caiman also provides protection against more advanced threats such as explosively formed penetrators. The armour package can be further enhanced with add-on panels. The vehicle is powered by a Caterpillar C7 turbo-diesel engine driving through an automatic transmission and features an all-wheel drive. A central tyre inflation system is also provided and operated from the cab. The Caiman can mount the M246, M2 Browning or Mk 19 in an armoured glass turret and can also be fitted with remote weapons stations. The Caiman entered service with the Marines Corps in 2007 and was also tested for use by the US Army.

Caiman MTV

This is basically an upgraded version of the 6x6 Caiman MRAP, which was designed specifically for use in Afghanistan. First demonstrated to the US Army in January 2010, a contract was subsequently

The Caiman MRAPs on patrol in Afghanistan. Note the distinctive sloped bonnet (hood) and small side windows. (Anita VanderMolen, US Army, Public domain, via Wikimedia Commons)

awarded to BAE for some 1,700 units. The armoured hull from the Caiman MRAP received an improved underbody protection kit while the suspension and power train were also upgraded. The vehicle was powered by a Caterpillar C9 Heavy Duty turbo diesel 6-cylinder engine driving through a 6-speed auto transmission. Coupled with its robust independent suspension, this gave the MTV improved mobility to tackle Afghanistan's rugged terrain. An enhanced climate/temperature control system was also fitted to improve crew comfort. The same armament fit was available as for the original Caiman, including provision for a remote weapon station.

Caiman MRAP Specifications	
Model	Caiman
Manufacturer	BAE Systems
Country	US
Year	2007
Engine	Caterpillar C7 370hp, (C9 400hp for MTV)
Fuel	Diesel
Transmission	Caterpillar CX28 6-speed auto
Suspension	Fully independent coil sprung
Top Speed	65mph
Range	370 miles
Armament	7.62 M240, 12.7 HMG or Mk 19 40mm GMG
Crew Capacity	10+1 (MTV)
Weight	20.8 tons (MRAP)

RG33

The RG33 is based on the South African RG31 and Mamba APC, developed by BAE with additional armour protection and improved mobility. Built in both 4x4 and 6x6 configurations, it is classed as a Medium MRAP by the US Marines and Army. Similar to other MRAPs, it features a V-shaped monocoque hull for blast protection. The engine compartment is a separate bolt-on armoured capsule and additional appliqué armour can be fitted if required. One notable feature of the vehicle is the

An RG33 MRAP pictured at Aberdeen Proving Ground in the US. The raised V-shaped underbelly is designed to deflect blasts. (US Navy Petty Officer 2nd Class Molly A. Burgess, Public domain, via Wikimedia Commons)

extensive use of armoured glass for the side windows. The 4x4 version can carry four plus two crew, while the larger 6x6 has the capacity for 8 plus 2. All crew and passengers are provided with blast attenuated seating and enter via the rear ramp. Available in several different versions, the RG33 can be configured as an infantry carrier, ambulance, command and control and engineer vehicle. A roof-mounted weapons ring enables the mounting of the usual weapon systems, and the vehicle can also be fitted with a remote weapons station.

RG33 Specifications	
Model	RG33 Troop Carrier
Manufacturer	BAE Systems
Country	US
Year	2007
Engine	Cummins 400hp
Fuel	Diesel
Transmission	Auto
Suspension	Fully independent coil sprung
Top Speed	105kph (road)
Range	N/A
Armament	7.62 M240, 12.7 HMG or Mk 19 40mm GMG
Crew Capacity	2+4
Weight	14 tons

Armoured Vehicles

M1117 Guardian ASV

Manufactured by Textron Marine and Land Systems, this 4x4 Armored Security Vehicle (ASV) was developed from the V150 LAV. This in turn was derived from the earlier Cadillac Gage Commando Armored Car produced in the 1970s. Initially designated the M117, it featured a V-shaped mine-resistant hull and was specifically designed for use in Iraq and Afghanistan with their high threat of IEDs. An additional appliqué composite armour package was also available to increase protection levels if required. In May 2011, Textron was initially awarded a contract by the US Army to supply 240 MSVs for the Afghan National Army (ANA), along with spares and support equipment. The MSV can additionally be fitted with an armoured turret housing a 12.7 Browning M2 HMG and 40mm Mk 19 Grenade Launcher, though it is not clear how many of the Afghan-supplied vehicles were so equipped. The Mobile Strike Force variant of the M1117 features all-wheel drive, an automatic transmission, air conditioning, and a central tyre-inflation system, giving it excellent mobility. These well-protected armoured vehicles were used to equip the Mobile Strike Forces – highly mobile, quick-reaction units assigned to regional commands within the ANA. The US government awarded further contracts to Textron to supply up to 634 ASVs in total, although it is not known how many of these were delivered before the final pull-out. It is worth noting the M1117 was also employed by the US Military Police and both a command and control and recovery version were available.

Guardian MSV Specifications	
Model	M1117
Manufacturer	Textron
Country	US
Year	1999
Engine	Cummins 6CTA8.3 260hp
Fuel	Diesel
Range	475 miles
Transmission	Allison MD3560 6-speed auto
Suspension	4x4 fully independent
Top Speed	70 mph (road)
Armament	7.62mm M240 plus 12.7mm Browning M2
Crew Capacity	Driver+8 dismounts
Weight	20 tons

The M1117 Guardian was developed from the Vietnam-era Cadillac Gage Commando, featuring a V-shaped mine-resistant hull. (MSGT Bert Mau, Public domain, via Wikimedia Commons)

Above left: The M1117s turret can mount a 7.62mm machine gun and 40mm automatic grenade launcher. Alternatively, it can be paired with a .50 calibre heavy machine gun. (Army.mil, Public domain, via Wikimedia Commons)

Above right: An M1117 pictured at a FOB – this gives a good impression of the size of the vehicle and its low silhouette compared to the MRAPs. (Army.mil, Public domain, via Wikimedia Commons)

Right: A pair of M1117 Mobile Strike Vehicles (MSVs) on patrol. Note the lead vehicle turret has been replaced with the O-GPK type. (DVIDSHUB, Public domain, via Wikimedia Commons)

A M1117 Guardian in US service. Note the side-mounted crew door and rear antenna mounting. (https://www.dvidshub.net/image/32527, Public domain, via Wikimedia Commons)

Above left: A column of MP M1117s on exercise in the US. Note the front-mounted winch and prominent feed chute for the 40mm grenade launcher. (Sgt 1st Class Roy Henry, Public domain, via Wikimedia Commons)

Above right: M1777 ASV on patrol in Afghanistan. Note the turret-mounted grenade launchers and prominent rear-mounted antennas. (Spc Micah E. Clare, US Army, Public domain, via Wikimedia Commons)

M113A2 APC

Essentially this is the familiar US Armored Personnel Carrier (APC) of Vietnam fame, originally developed in the 1960s but modified and updated over the years to keep it current. Replaced in front-line service by the Bradley Infantry Fighting Vehicle (IFV), significant numbers are still used by the US Army in support roles. The M113 has also been widely supplied to America's allies and is currently in use by Israel, Canada, Australia, Taiwan, South Korea and Pakistan, to name but a few. One of the first AFVs to use aluminium armour in its construction, the A2 version came into service in 1979. This enhanced model includes better cooling for the 215bhp 6V-53 Detroit Diesel engine, an improved torsion bar suspension setup and armoured fuel tanks. This increased the all-up weight to 11,740kg, and the A2 lacks the amphibious capability of the earlier version. The later A4 version features an extra

An M113A4 providing convoy escort for a CLP in Helmand. Note the additional stowage and numerous antennas for communications and ECM equipment.

road wheel and lengthened hull for more internal space. The M577 variant is simply an M113 series APC with a higher roof to the rear of the driver's position. The hull is still of all-welded aluminium armour, providing the occupants with protection from small arms fire and shell splinters. The M577 series was designed as a CP or 'command post' variant, with greater room for radio equipment and its operators. Although lacking high levels of protection from IEDs and large calibre weapons, the M113 series is still useful as a 'battlefield taxi' and has good cross-country performance. In Iraq and Afghanistan, these vehicles received additional slat armour and were sometimes fitted with an armoured turret. Up to 189 examples of both types were supplied to the Afghan military, but it is unknown how many remain in serviceable condition in Taliban hands.

M113 Specifications	
Model	M113A2 APC
Manufacturer	United Defence
Country	US
Year	1979
Engine	6V53T, 6-cylinder
Fuel	Diesel
Range	330 miles
Transmission	6-speed manual
Suspension	Torsion bar
Top Speed	42mph
Armament	12.7mm Browning M2
Capacity	5 plus
Weight	12.3 tons

The classic M113 APC has served from Vietnam to the Gulf War and still finds a role with US support units. (DoD photo by Staff Sgt Shane A. Cuomo, US Air Force, Public domain, via Wikimedia Commons)

Above: This later updated model features prominent rear sponsons. Note the claymore mines attached to the side armour. (Captain Jason McCree, USAF, Public domain, via Wikimedia Commons)

Left: An M113 rear ramp and interior with basic seating for infantry dismounts. Note the large roof hatch. (Yellowute at English Wikipedia, Public domain, via Wikimedia Commons)

Australian M113s from a cavalry unit. This Cold War veteran is still proving useful on the modern battlefield and has recently been supplied to Ukraine. (LSIS Andrew Dakin, Public domain, via Wikimedia Commons)

Stryker ICV

The Striker is a hybrid APC/infantry fighting vehicle based on the Canadian LAV III and built for the US Army. Stryker is actually a family of vehicles, which equip the rapid deployment Brigade Combat Teams. An eight-wheeled design like the Mowag Piranha, the Stryker comes in ten variants including infantry carrier, commander post, ambulance, fire support, engineer, anti-tank guided missile carrier, mortar carrier, reconnaissance vehicle, mobile gun system and NBC reconnaissance vehicle. The Stryker was first employed operationally in the Iraq War of 2003, which highlighted a number of issues with the design. The levels of protection had been found inadequate and were improved with the introduction of slat armour and reactive armour tiles to counter the RPG threat. The hull was also reshaped to a V-configuration to deflect the blast from mines and IEDs. The V-shaped hull was not available for all models and the extra weight required further suspension upgrades. The original C7 Caterpillar 350hp engine was superseded by a more powerful 450hp version in later models to improve mobility. Despite the extra protection offered by the V-shaped hull, the tight driver compartment of these versions was to cause problems in operational use, prompting a further redesign. There remained concerns about vulnerability to IEDs, although the Stryker proved superior to many other US designs in use in Afghanistan.

The main armament of the Stryker is the M151 remote weapon station mounting a 7.62mm M240 MG, 12.7mm M2 Browning HMG or 40mm Mk 19 Grenade Launcher. The MGS version of the Stryker is armed with a 30mm cannon housed in a Kongsberg Medium Caliber Remote Weapons Station and trials have been carried out to mount Javelin ATGWs. The vehicle is air portable by C130 and C17 transport aircraft in keeping with the Stryker Brigade's intervention and rapid deployment role. It relies on its speed and manoeuvrability on the conventional battlefield rather than heavy armour. Initially plagued by a series of reliability issues, the Stryker has been steadily upgraded over the years and still has a place in the US inventory.

A dramatic image of a Stryker ICV at speed during mobility testing. (US Army, Public domain, via Wikimedia Commons)

Stryker Specifications	
Model	Stryker ICF
Manufacturer	General Dynamics Land Systems
Country	US
Year	2002
Engine	Caterpillar C7 350hp
Fuel	Diesel
Range	310 miles
Transmission	Allison 3200SP auto
Suspension	8x8
Top Speed	60mph (road)
Armament	7.62mm, 12.7mm Browning M2, 40mm Mk 19 GMG, (30mm Cannon, MGS)
Crew Capacity	2+9 (troop carrier)
Weight	16.4 tons

Left: American soldiers de-bus from their Stryker troop carrier. Note the jerrycans stowed at the rear and remote weapons station for the 12.7mm M2 Browning. (US Army, Public domain, via Wikimedia Commons)

Below: Strykers patrol alongside dismounted troops; these examples are equipped with remote weapons stations and a full suite of slat armour. (US Army, Public domain, via Wikimedia Commons)

US Vehicles

Above left: A typically equipped Troop Carrier pictured in Afghanistan, fitted with slat armour and a cam-net covered sun canopy. (MCC Bill Mesta, Public domain, via Wikimedia Commons)

Above right: This image gives a good view of the remote weapons station for the .5 HMG, which features a searchlight and clusters of grenade dischargers. (TSgt Mike Buytas, USAF, Public domain, via Wikimedia Commons)

Right: A Stryker operating in southern Afghanistan. Note the spare wheel carried on the top deck and open roof hatches. (TSgt Mike Buytas, USAF, Public domain, via Wikimedia Commons)

US troops deploy from a Stryker equipped with slat armour and a full communications and ECM fit. Note the prominent sun canopy and ration boxes stored behind the slat armour. (DoD photo by Staff Sgt Shane Hamann, US Army (Released), Public domain, via Wikimedia Commons)

LAV-25

The LAV-25 is based on the Canadian AVGP family of wheeled armoured vehicles, which in turn are based on the Swiss Piranha. Built in Canada by General Dynamics Land Systems, the vehicles are produced for the US Marines Corps. The US Army preferred to develop the similar Stryker, although a small number of LAVs have been used as reconnaissance vehicles by the 82nd Airborne Division and selective armoured units. The LAV is relatively lightly armoured, relying on speed and manoeuvrability to keep it out of trouble. Power is provided by a 6V53T 300hp turbo-diesel engine driving through an Allison auto transmission. There is a selective 8x8 and 8x4 drive available; the latter is used to extend the range on long road moves. There is also a central tyre inflation system, and the vehicle has a good cross-country capability. The LAV-25 is fitted with a welded armoured turret that houses the 25mm M242 Bushmaster chain-gun with co-axial 7.62mm M240C MG. There is also provision for an additional pintle-mounted M240B machine gun. There are several variants of the basic vehicle including command, mortar carrier, recovery, logistics plus an anti-tank version armed with TOW missiles. The troop carrier has a three-man crew and can accommodate 6 dismounts in the rear compartment. The armour is sufficient to protect against 7.62mm small arms and shell splinters with the thicker frontal area proof against 12.7mm rounds. Operational experience in Iraq and Afghanistan led to a programme to up-armour the LAV, with the improved LAV-25A2 featuring additional protection up to 14.5mm with the fitting of armoured tiles. This version also included uprated suspension, improved fire suppression and a new thermal sighting system. The LAV-25 is fully amphibious with minimal preparation. It is also air portable by USAF transport aircraft and can be carried under-slung by heavy-lift helicopters. The vehicle also has the distinction of being capable of insertion by parachute if required. The LAV has served the Marines well but is now long in the tooth and due for replacement. Despite this, it is expected to soldier on well into the 2020s.

Marines resting beside their heavily loaded LAV. Note the additional spare wheel mounted at the rear and rucksacks attached to the sides. (Public domain, via Wikimedia Commons)

This shot gives a good impression of the turret with its 25mm Bushmaster cannon. Note the co-axial 7.62mm MG and grenade dischargers. (Sgt Randall Clinton, Public domain, via Wikimedia Commons)

LAV-25 Specifications

Model	LAV25/LAV-25A2
Manufacturer	General Dynamics Land Systems
Country	US
Year	1983
Engine	6V53T 300hp
Fuel	Diesel
Range	410 miles
Transmission	Allison MT653 5-speed auto
Suspension	8x8
Top Speed	62mph (road)
Armament	M242 25mm Bushmaster Chain Gun plus co-axial 7.62mm MG
Crew Capacity	3+6
Weight	12.8 tons

Above left: US Marines on patrol with their LAV-25 in Kandahar Province. Note the recovery cable carried on the front glacis plate. (US Marine Corps photo by Cpl Randall A. Clinton, Public domain, via Wikimedia Commons)

Above right: A LAV-25 operating in Afghanistan. Note the prominent tubular antennas, which are part of the ECM fit. (Public domain, via Wikimedia Commons)

Left: A typical US Marine LAV-25. The vehicle is similar in concept to the US Army Stryker but features a prominent turret mounting a M242 25mm Bushmaster Chain Gun. (Alvaro Aro, US Marine Corps, Public domain, via Wikimedia Commons)

Right: A pair of LAVs operating in Helmand. Note the plethora of antennas for communications and ECM equipment and pre-mounted recovery cables. (DVIDSHUB, Public domain, via Wikimedia Commons)

Logistics Vehicles

Navistar 7000 MV

Produced by Navistar International and based on a commercial truck chassis, this 4x6 logistics vehicle has a payload of 4½ tons. Powered by a 7.6-litre turbo diesel engine, it is an ideal heavy-hauler and comes in several configurations. These include cargo, tanker and recovery versions. The US government ordered some 14,000 of these trucks for use by the Afghan National Army and Police.

Navistar 7000 Specifications	
Model	Medium Truck
Manufacturer	Navistar Defence
Country	US
Year	2005
Engine	International DT530 270-330hp
Fuel	Diesel
Range	400 miles
Transmission	Auto
Suspension	Parabolic leaf
Top Speed	N/A
Crew Capacity	3
Weight	10.2 tons

Thousands of these Navistar 7000 trucks were supplied to Afghan security forces in several different versions. (Sgt Rachael K. A. Moore, Public domain, via Wikimedia Commons)

Oshkosh MTV

Produced by Oshkosh and BAE Systems, these Medium Tactical Vehicles (MTVs) are based on an Austrian Steyr design, modified to meet US requirements. Powered by a 7.2-litre, 6-cylinder inline diesel developing 275bhp and fitted with a 7-speed automatic transmission, they have a payload of up to 5 US tons. With an operational range of 300 miles, these are excellent load haulers and, as every logistics officer knows, trucks like these are vital to an army's supply chain. More than 8,000 of these trucks were supplied to the Afghan forces over the years, but it is not known how many remain serviceable.

Oshkosh Medium Truck Specifications	
Model	Oshkosh MTV
Manufacturer	Oshkosh Defence
Country	US
Year	2005
Engine	Caterpillar C7 275hp
Fuel	Diesel
Range	300 miles
Transmission	7-speed auto
Suspension	Parabolic leaf springs
Top Speed	58mph
Crew Capacity	2
Weight	11 tons

The Oshkosh MTV is a medium truck with 5-ton payload, supplied to the Afghan military in large numbers. Note the distinctive armoured cab and belly plate. (http://oshkoshdefense.co.uk, CC BY-SA 4.0 https://creativecommons.org/licenses/by-sa/4.0, via Wikimedia Commons)

M1249 MRV Wrecker

This heavy-duty wrecker was specifically designed to recover MRAPs, hence MRV (MRAP Recovery Vehicle). Designed by Navistar, it is one of the heaviest vehicles in the US inventory and features a 30-ton large capacity boom capable of front or rear recovery. Combined with its two 20,000lb winches and 50,000lb drag winch, the M1249 can recover the largest of vehicles. Some 250 of these Wreckers were ordered for use in Afghanistan.

MRV Specifications	
Model	M1249 Wrecker
Manufacturer	Navistar Defence
Country	US
Year	2010
Engine	6-cylinder 375hp
Fuel	Diesel
Range	600km
Transmission	Allison auto
Suspension	N/A
Top Speed	105kph (road)
Crew Capacity	2

The M1249 Wrecker was specifically designed to recover damaged MRAPs and can handle the heaviest vehicles in the US inventory. (Sgt Scott Davis, Public domain, via Wikimedia Commons)

Chapter 3

Aftermath

Like other Afghan veterans, I watched in horror at the precipitate US withdrawal and removal of air cover and technical support that led to the rapid collapse of the Afghan Army. The impotence of President Mohammed Shia's government in the face of the insurgents and the speed of their advance surprised everyone, even the Taliban themselves. Desperate scenes of Afghans crowding Kabul Airport were flashed on the evening news and were sometimes hard to watch as the evacuation gathered pace. In purely technical terms, this mass evacuation might be termed a success but, as Churchill famously said, wars are not won by evacuations. The War on Terror goes on with deployments to Syria, Mali and the Sahel, although the term is no longer popular with our American allies. The one positive I draw from this whole sad affair is the performance of my former colleagues within the 16 Air Assault Brigade, who did an almost impossible job in the most difficult of circumstances. Never was the Parachute Regiments motto, *Utrinque Paratus* (Ready for Anything), more apt, and I allowed myself a brief glow of pride. After a 20-year war, Western forces are now out of Afghanistan, apparently for good, ceding the country to the Taliban. Perhaps the most worrying feature of this rapid departure is actually what has been left behind. Since 2005, the US has spent some US$18bn supporting the Afghan military and the hardware this money bought is now in the hands of the Taliban. The haul includes thousands of small arms and hundreds of armoured vehicles, along with a small air force. The scale of all this is staggering, including Humvees, a substantial fleet of trucks and thousands of Ford pickup trucks. More worrying still are all the armoured vehicles and heavy weapons that will make the Taliban one of the most potent military forces in the region. The sight of Taliban Special Forces parading in captured US equipment and carrying M4 carbines underlined the fact that this is no longer a group of rag-tag insurgents armed with worn-out Kalashnikovs.

In addition to the thousands of armoured and soft-skinned vehicles supplied since 2003, it is estimated the US has supplied the Afghan military with at least 600,000 infantry weapons, a truly staggering figure. The majority of these have been M16 rifles and M4 carbines, along with large numbers of 7.62mm and 12.7mm machine guns. Then there is all the ammunition and munitions supplied over the years. Just to give an indication of the scale of this, between 2017 and 2019, the US supplied 7,035 machine guns, 20,040 hand grenades, 2,520 bombs and 1,394 grenade launchers. In addition, some 162,000 pieces of communication equipment, and 16,000 night-vision goggle devices have been gifted to the Afghan military, along with body armour, helmets, boots, uniforms and personal equipment. You might think this is an impressive cache to have fallen into the Taliban's lap and you would be right. You might also consider that this does not include all the ex-Soviet equipment, including artillery pieces, APCs and T55 and T62 Main Battle Tanks, now in their hands. The sheer scale of expenditure, some US$83bn since 2003 is perhaps only possible if you are the world's largest economy. However, US taxpayers must surely now be asking themselves if this was money well spent. What is more worrying is what happens to all this US-supplied ordinance in the future, as it may be passed onto other terrorist organisations. Alternatively, the Taliban may sell off some of this hardware to the highest bidder in return for the hard cash they need to prop up a failing economy. Either way, it bodes ill for the West and is the largest haul of military equipment to fall into the hands of an enemy since the Communists defeat of South Vietnam.

An Afghan soldier trains with a Browning M2 HMG. Large quantities of US-supplied small arms were left behind. (Lance Cpl Darien Bjorndal, Public domain, via Wikimedia Commons)

Left: Some of the thousands of MRAPs supplied to the former Afghan government over the years. (MSgt Benjamin Bloker, Public domain, via Wikimedia Commons)

Below: Several A29 Super Tucano light attack aircraft were abandoned at Kabul Airport after the withdrawal. (Member of US Air Force, Public domain, via Wikimedia Commons)

Chapter 4

Operation *Pitting*, Escape from Kabul

The US withdrawal and the subsequent rapid collapse of Afghan government forces that followed created an unprecedented humanitarian crisis centred on the international airport in Kabul. Thousands of Western nationals along with dependants and desperate Afghans crowded the gates in chaotic scenes. Among those trying to escape were UK nationals, interpreters and others who had worked for the British. In this febrile atmosphere, the government turned to 16 Air Assault Brigade, the British Army's key rapid deployment unit. Central to the mission would be the Paratroopers of 2 and 3 Para, who maintained a high level of readiness to deploy anywhere in the world. The Brigade's current lead element or Air Manoeuvre Battle Group (AMBG) was led by 2 Para, which was on summer leave when the crisis blew up. Recalled to duty, they were all back at their Colchester barracks and ready to deploy within 12 hours, an impressive feat. Initial briefings indicated several potential threats, including suicide bombers, mortar and artillery fire and confrontation with the Taliban. Troops were warned they should be prepared to fight, although the aim was to avoid direct

RAF C17 on the flight line at Kabul Airport prepares to pick up evacuees. (16 Air Assault Brigade)

Afghan refugees board an RAF transport aircraft early in the evacuation. (16 Air Assault Brigade)

Above: A line-up of RAF and USAF C-17s about to take on passengers. (16 Air Assault Brigade)

Left: Paratroopers take a brief rest between shifts at the entrance gates. (16 Air Assault Brigade)

combat and to facilitate the evacuation. On 14 August, Operation *Pitting* was launched, with some 650 troops from the Brigade, along with Special Forces plus a contingent from the Special Forces Support Group (1 Para). The mission was led by Brigadier Dan Blanchard and the force was deployed into theatre by air transport provided by the RAF.

As luck would have it, this kind of Service Protected Evacuation had long been a feature of the Paras training, as I remember from my own time with the regiment. However, the scenario existing in Kabul with the Taliban controlling all access to the airport was one the planners had never envisaged. The Special Forces group landed at Kabul during the night of Friday, 13 August, and were briefed by intelligence officers based at the British Embassy. They would work closely with US Special Forces in the coming days to help rescue UK nationals and others trapped in the city. The 2 Para Battle Group, along with the Pathfinders, began arriving the following morning and immediately began assisting American forces to secure the airport. There were some 4,500 US troops already in place, made up of Marines and

Above left: 3 Para soldier checking refugees' passports at the holding area. (16 Air Assault Brigade)

Above right: An Afghan presents his papers to a Paratrooper manning the gates. (16 Air Assault Brigade)

Right: 2 Para quickly made use of abandoned transport found at the airport. (16 Air Assault Brigade)

Paratroopers. The latter belonged to the 82nd Airborne, with which the Parachute Regiment maintains close links, aiding liaison on the ground. The Hotel Baron close to the airport perimeter was occupied early on and had already been used by the Americans to ferry out their nationals by helicopter.

In the early phase of the evacuation, with the city in chaos and the Taliban yet to exert full control, the Paratroopers were able to leave the airport to search for people. The scene is described by a 2 Para soldier, 'It's crazy out here, within two hours of touching down in Kabul we had taken to the streets to rescue people. Everyone from 2 Para landed and went straight into it; we had no choice. It was really chaotic as Kabul was falling.' The majority of UK nationals were picked up that first day and consisted mainly of ex-pats, those working with NGOs and contractors.

Evacuees were brought to the airfield using vehicles abandoned at the airport. They were then fed and given the chance to rest but as one of the soldiers said, 'conditions were basic, while most were just relieved to be getting out'. By the night of Sunday, 15 August, Kabul had effectively fallen, and the Taliban began to exert closer control over access to the airport. By midday on Monday, 2 Para had safely conducted the first evacuation, with around 200 British nationals flying out by RAF transport aircraft.

Above left: The emotional strain of dealing with desperate Afghans is etched on this Paratrooper's face. (16 Air Assault Brigade)

Above right: UK Ambassador Sir Laurie Bristow chats with members of 3 Para at the airport. (16 Air Assault Brigade)

Left: The Paratroopers begin to leave Kabul as the evacuation draws to a close. (16 Air Assault Brigade)

Meanwhile, the rescue of interpreters and Afghan staff who had worked for the British was begun under the Afghan Relocation and Assistance Policy (ARAP) scheme. By Tuesday, crowds of desperate Afghans had gathered at the airport entrances. 'It's chaos. People are fighting for their lives to get in and British soldiers are at the front of it', explained a 2 Para soldier. By now, the Taliban had set up a ring of checkpoints on the approaches to the airport and were making life increasingly difficult for those trying to escape. Those who had reached the airport were becoming increasingly desperate, pleading with the soldiers to be let in and waving their documents. The strain on the soldiers was immense and there were chaotic scenes as they tried to identify those who were eligible for evacuation. In the end, Paratroopers are trained to deal with chaos and, gradually, some order was established, with holding areas set up to process the evacuees. Meanwhile, Taliban fighters were sometimes stationed only a few feet away at the entrance gates, which one paratrooper described as a surreal experience after 20 years of war. The worry at this stage, however, was not so much the Taliban, but the desperation of people fleeing for their lives. As former Defence Chief Lord Richards said at the time, 'UK forces securing the airstrip are in a "very precarious situation", with little protection from security threats posed by the likes of the so-called Islamic State. This is the worst possible scenario when you are unable to clear a space between the airhead and your possible threat, which is exactly what is happening now.'

Above left: Commander of 16 Air Assault Brigade, Brigadier James Martin is greeted by Air Commodore David Manning on his return. (16 Air Assault Brigade)

Above right: An SNCO from 3 Para manages a smile after returning safely to RAF Brize Norton. (16 Air Assault Brigade)

Right: Dramatic scenes as Paratroopers pluck a child from the crowds of Afghans waiting to gain entry to the airport. (16 Air Assault Brigade)

The difficult situation on the ground left the troops hard-pressed and it was decided to bring in reinforcements, with an additional company from 3 Para arriving by Thursday, 19 August. Evacuation flights were now starting to leave regularly, with the RAF employing its C130Js, and A400M tactical transports along with the giant C17 Globemasters. In one of the early flights, a pilot narrowly missed a bus blocking his take-off run, while one C17 took off with a total of 439 passengers on board, a record for an RAF aircraft. By now, as one soldier described, the troops had developed 'a really good system to transition chaos'. Despite this, tragic scenes were played out in front of the world's media. In an emotional piece to camera, veteran correspondent Stuart Ramsey reported, 'Paratroopers began pulling people from the mayhem, medics rushing from the next casualty to the next, then the next and the next, crushed, dehydrated, terrified'. Soldiers started shouting for medics and stretchers as unconscious people were carried to the rear. It was at this point that people were finally being successfully processed and, by 20 August, the troops had evacuated more than 2,400 people, 599 of them UK nationals.

Above left: The cavernous hold of a C-17 crammed with hundreds of fleeing Afghans. (16 Air Assault Brigade)

Above right: A paratrooper spares some time for the children among all the chaos. (16 Air Assault Brigade)

The pressure at the gates remained relentless and the Taliban was now turning people back, even those with papers. There were also disturbing reports of Taliban hunting down former government officials, and many eligible Afghans became stuck behind a web of Taliban checkpoints lining the route to the airport. There was frustration that the operation was so last minute, but with little sign that the Taliban would extend the 31 August deadline, the troops just got on with it. It was at this point the photograph of a British Paratrooper clutching a small child hit the front pages of the British newspapers and was beamed around the world. It underlined the emotional strain the troops were under, and as Armed Forces Minister James Heappey said, British troops are 'seeing things that are unimaginably hard to deal with', as reports continued of overcrowding and violence in the Kabul heat. The soldiers had the difficult job of turning people away at the gates, unable to take those lacking the correct documentation. It was a heartbreaking task, even for hardened Paratroopers.

As the Taliban net steadily tightened, operations were largely confined to the international airport and nearby Baron Hotel. However, with UK and Western nationals still stranded in the city and blocked by Taliban checkpoints, an operation was mounted to rescue them. Conducted by SAS operators assisted by Paratroopers from the Special Forces Support Group, the mission was conducted at the dead of night when the Taliban was thinner on the ground. Using abandoned vehicles from the British Embassy, Special Forces teams fanned out across the city to locate and rescue UK citizens. Several foreign nationals were also picked up in the sweeps and brought back to the Baron Hotel for processing. Despite reports that US forces were against mounting operations outside the wire, the US did assist with

Above left: Mission accomplished, a C-17 RAF transport flies out of Kabul with soldiers from 2 Para. (16 Air Assault Brigade)

Above right: 2 Para practise a Service Protected Evacuation during an exercise. (16 Air Assault Brigade)

intelligence and the mission seems to have been largely successful. One US reporter trapped in the city spoke of her perilous journey to escape, assisted by a window of opportunity provided by British Special Forces troops. Susannah George from the *Washington Post* explained she was only able to reach her flight after British soldiers arrived to evacuate her and her compatriots from a safe house in the city.

With the Taliban deadline of 31 August fast looming, the evacuation took on a new sense of urgency, with 731 people processed for UK flights on Sunday morning alone. Then, in the early evening of 26 August, news came of what everyone had feared, with a bomb detonated at the entrance to the airport. The explosion occurred beside a drainage canal where US troops were busy checking people's documents and 13 Marines and 169 Afghan civilians were killed in the blast. British soldiers immediately rushed to the scene to offer what assistance they could and to help with the wounded. Subsequent responsibility for the attack was claimed by the militant group Islamic State-Khorasan Province, which had infiltrated a suicide bomber into the crowds of evacuees. It was a chilling reminder of the vulnerability of both soldiers and civilians alike. Despite the increasing risks, evacuation flights continued, although as Defence Secretary Ben Wallace stated, 'absolutely nobody can say we'll be able to get everybody out', as the UK pressed for more time. In the end, it was not to be, and the UK effort began winding down, with the last civilian flight leaving on 28 August. After that, the effort was solely concentrated on withdrawing British diplomatic and service personnel. Since 14 August, the RAF had made some 165 round trips from the UK, rescuing almost 1,500 UK nationals and Afghan civilians. It was the largest humanitarian airlift that British forces had ever conducted, although, inevitably, given the tight deadline, many entitled Afghans had to be left behind. Still, at least some measure of success could be claimed to set against the tragic end of Britain's 20-year engagement in Afghanistan. As for the troops, they had done a magnificent job in the most difficult of circumstances.

This image of a Paratrooper with a small child was beamed around the world and hit the front pages. (16 Air Assault Brigade)

Paratroopers man one of the holding areas close to the gates. (16 Air Assault Brigade)

These Afghans were lucky and had managed to find a place on a flight out. (16 Air Assault Brigade)

A 2 Para soldier oversees crowds of Afghans hoping for a flight to freedom. (16 Air Assault Brigade)

Units that took part
2 Para, 3 Para, 1 Para SFSG, Pathfinders, 22 SAS (A Squadron)
Note: 16 AA Bde provided medics, engineers and an RMP detachment.

RAF aircraft used in the airlift
C-130J Hercules: The famous 'Herc' formed the backbone of RAF air transport for many decades and remains a highly effective aircraft. The standard C-130J is the latest model of this veteran air lifter and the RAF operate 14 of the stretched C-130J-30 version, now designated the Hercules C4. These aircraft are currently to be retired in 2023, with their role being taken over by the larger C400M.

C400M Atlas: The Atlas was the result of a joint European venture to design a new tactical transport. The RAF currently operates 20 of these impressive aircraft, with a further two on order. Capable of operating from rough strips, they are larger and have a greater payload than the C130J, which they are to replace.

Boeing C-17 Globemaster: The RAF originally leased four of these heavy lift jet transports but subsequently decided to buy them outright. They now operate a fleet of eight of these strategic air transports, which are capable of carrying personnel or freight and feature a huge cargo bay that can swallow an entire Chinook helicopter.

A330 Voyager: These aircraft are the long-haul version of the Airbus A330, adapted to meet RAF requirements. They can carry personnel, freight or a mixed cargo and a number have been modified to act as air-refuelling tankers. The RAF currently operates a fleet of 14 of these multi-role aircraft, which took over from the earlier VC10s and Tristars.

Note: Operation *Pitting* was the UK's largest mass airlift since the Berlin Airlift of 1948.

Other books you might like:

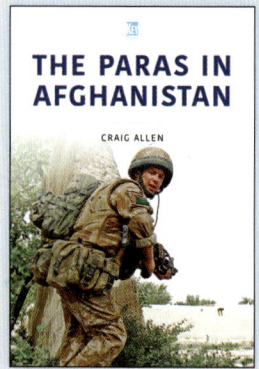
Modern Wars Series, Vol. 2

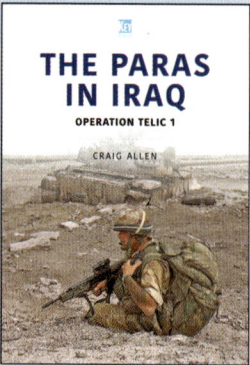
Modern Wars Series, Vol. 1

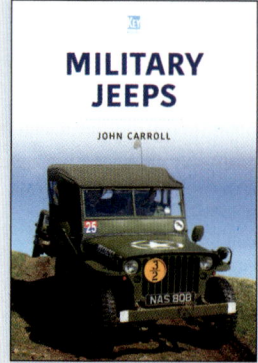
Military Vehicles and Artillery Series, Vol. 3

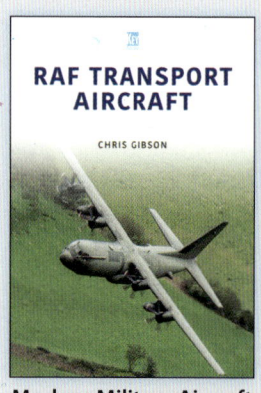
Modern Military Aircraft Series, Vol. 6

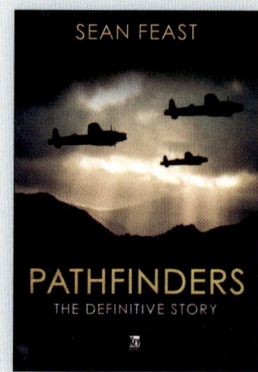

For our full range of titles please visit:
shop.keypublishing.com/books

VIP Book Club

Sign up today and receive
TWO FREE E-BOOKS

Be the first to find out about our forthcoming book releases and receive exclusive offers.

Register now at **keypublishing.com/vip-book-club**

Our VIP Book Club is a 100% spam-free zone, and we will never share your email with anyone else. You can read our full privacy policy at: privacy.keypublishing.com